eBay Motors the Smart Way

Selling and Buying Cars, Trucks, Motorcycles, Boats, Parts, Accessories, and Much More on the Web's #1 Auction Site

Joseph T. Sinclair

and

Don Spillane

American Management Association
New York • Atlanta • Brussels • Chicago • Mexico City • San Francisco
Shanghai • Tokyo • Toronto • Washington, D.C.

Special discounts on bulk quantities of AMACOM books are available to corporations, professional associations, and other organizations. For details, contact Special Sales Department, AMACOM, a division of American Management Association, 1601 Broadway, New York, NY 10019.
Tel.: 212-903-8316. Fax: 212-903-8083.

This publication is designed to provide accurate and authoritative information in regard to the subject matter covered. It is sold with the understanding that the publisher is not engaged in rendering legal, accounting, or other professional service. If legal advice or other expert assistance is required, the services of a competent professional person should be sought.

Library of Congress Cataloging-in-Publication Data

Sinclair, Joseph T.
  eBay motors the smart way : selling and buying cars, trucks, motorcycles, boats, parts, accessories, and much more on the web's #1 auction site / Joseph T. Sinclair, Don Spillane.—1st ed.
     p. cm.
     Includes bibliographical references and index.
     ISBN 0-8144-7252-4
     1. Internet auctions. 2. Automobile auctions—Computer network resources. 3. eBay (Firm) I. Spillane, Don. II. Title.
  HF5478.S472004
  381'.456292—dc22   2003027336
                                                             CIP

Printing number
10 9 8 7 6 5 4 3 2 1

To my Michigan relatives and friends, especially to my uncle and aunt, William Patrick Connolly and Dorothy Margaret Hoener Connolly, and my cousins, Kathleen Grace Connolly Rogers, William Patrick Connolly, Jr., and Carol Miriam Connolly Anderson; to my friends Herman and Ernestine Shelton, and their son John L. Shelton and his wife Margaret Mauer Shelton; and to my relatives and friends who worked in the automotive industry including my grandfather Albert L. Hoener, uncle William P. Connolly, cousin Dale L. Prentice, friend Douglas Zahn, and my parents' life-long friends George I. Connely and Irving Brown, together with their wives Elizabeth Butler Connely and Jane Brown.

Joseph T. Sinclair

To my father Daniel J. Spillane and brother Dennis J. Spillane who left us too young and are missed every day.

Don Spillane

Contents

Acknowledgments

My first contact with eBay employees was in San Jose in September 1998 at the eBay third birthday party. Even at that time they were contemplating the creation of a special eBay market to sell vehicles. Oddly enough, it seemed to me a good idea at the time. And it was only two-and-a-half years later that I sold a vehicle on eBay Motors. Congratulations to the clever people at eBay who have done a super job of creating yet another new and effective online marketplace. Good work!

I also want to thank Munjal Shah, CEO of Andale a leading auction management service, for suggesting that I write an eBay Motors book. Another person I would like to thank and acknowledge is Victor Owens, master mechanic at Brooks Automotive in Vallejo, California, who did some homework for me to use in this book. Many thanks to Don Spillane, co-author, who introduced me to eBay in 1998 and who is the quintessential retailer on eBay, first selling collectibles and now selling Acuras and other high end cars.

Thanks also to Jacqueline Flynn, Executive Editor, and the folks at AMA-COM, including Mike Sivilli and Kama Timbrell, who contributed to this book with lots of energy; Andy Ambraziejus, Managing Editor, who among other important duties makes sure my books get published as ebooks; and Hank Kennedy, Publisher, and his entire staff who had the foresight to see that eBay is now a vast national enterprise that requires specialty books.

And thanks to my agent, Carole McClendon at Waterside Productions, who always does a reliable job of making things work. Finally, thanks to my wife Lani, daughter Brook, and son Tommy, who put up with the workaholic-writer dad.

Two experiences in my life have led to my interest in cars and particularly in buying cars frugally. The first was growing up in the Detroit area where cars are always a topic of conversation. The second was being around Herman Shelton, the father of my best friend, who never made a purchase that wasn't an example in frugality and who never bought a new car. Yet Herman always drove a fine car. Thanks, Herman.

This Acknowledgement shouldn't end without thanking all the readers who have supported *eBay the Smart Way*, now in its third edition, and *eBay Business the Smart Way*. Only the success of these two books have made it possible to write about a specialized eBay marketplace. The eBay Motors marketplace is now huge, and I hope readers will find reading this new book *eBay Motors the Smart Way* worthwhile and will also find their vehicle sales to be profitable and their purchases to be thrifty. Good luck!

Joseph T. Sinclair

Thanks to my wife Wendy and children Zack and Shannon who inspire me daily.

Don Spillane

I

Introducing eBay Motors

1

Introduction

Whether you're a buyer, seller, or dealer, eBay Motors is an exciting new marketplace for vehicles where you can save money and make money. Save money and make money? How can both happen at the same time in the same marketplace? Well, that's one of the great benefits of a large national marketplace. Everyone, whether buyer or seller, can do well financially or realize greater efficiency. But let's put that thought on hold for a minute while we review the numbers on eBay Motors.

In 2002 eBay members sold 300,000 vehicles on eBay Motors worth $3 billion. About 75 percent of those transactions took place across state lines. In 2003 eBay members sold about twice as many vehicles as in 2002 on eBay Motors, and in the fourth quarter of the year eBay Motors had annualized vehicle sales of $7.5 billion. So you can see that this is not a trivial market, and the information that follows is not theory. eBay works for both buyers and sellers.

Otherwise Successful

eBay, not just eBay Motors, is quite successful too. At the end of 2003, eBay had 95 million registered members and sales of $24 billion. In mid 2003 eBay had 16 million items for sale everyday and 27,000 categories of goods.

In the Second Edition of *eBay the Smart Way* in 2001 I said, "I'm bullish about eBay Motors. It will evolve into a dynamic vehicle marketplace over the next few years and gain a significant market share at the expense of local classifieds. It's doing well already." The figures now show that there was something to this prediction.

National Marketplace

Getting back to exploring the idea of a large national marketplace, let's look first at local markets. Local markets don't operate very efficiently. They're not large enough. For instance, you will pay more for a used car in Grand Junction, Colorado, than you will in Denver, Colorado. Grand Junction is simply a smaller city than Denver, about one-tenth the size. The number of cars available for sale in Grand Junction is smaller, and the dealers are fewer. The competition is less. Then too, there are fewer buyers, and they have fewer choices.

The cars being sold are likely to stay on the lot longer, overhead is therefore higher, and dealer confidence for turning over inventory quickly is likely not as high in Grand Junction as it is in Denver.

Dealer sales efficiency is likely to be less, and the cost of operating (per vehicle for sale) is likely to be higher in Grand Junction. This translates into higher prices in Grand Junction than in Denver.

General Statement

The statement about Grand Junction is a general statement based on population size and does not pertain to any specific dealership in Grand Junction.

In Grand Junction the higher prices for used cars clearly don't benefit buyers. But do they benefit dealers? The answer is "No." The dealers don't operate as efficiently as they could in a larger marketplace. They have to get higher prices to make a normal business profit.

Note that local dealers constitute the local marketplace for used vehicles. Although it's true that the classified ad section of the local newspaper has traditionally been another marketplace where individuals can buy and sell vehicles, typically it does not have nearly the volume of the marketplace made by local dealers. Being smaller, the classified ad marketplace is less efficient than the local dealer marketplace. Prices will tend to reflect the local dealer marketplace rather than a separate price structure.

Now, make the jump from the Denver used vehicle market to the national used vehicle marketplace. The national marketplace offers even lower prices to buyers but greater efficiencies to dealers. But how can you make that jump? There's no large national marketplace for used vehicles, is there? Well, there wasn't a large national marketplace for used vehicles until the Internet set the stage for one. But now it's there, and eBay Motors is the leader.

For instance, check the number of Chevrolet Camaros for sale in your locale. The number on eBay Motors each week is well over 400. Check the number of Cadillac DeVilles for sale locally. The number on eBay is well over 200 each week. No local market can match these numbers. This shows that the national marketplace is huge. A huge marketplace breeds competition and results in efficiencies. Both buyers and sellers get benefits from larger marketplaces. And eBay Motors is now the largest used car marketplace in the US.

Does it make sense to buy a used car in Chicago when you live in Denver? It does depending on what you're looking for. The market in large cities tends to be a little thin when you're looking for something specific. There are so many brands, so many models.

For instance, if you're looking for a used, midsize sedan, 1998–2000 model, in good condition in Denver, you won't have any trouble finding one. However, if instead you're looking for a used Ford Taurus, 2000 model, with leather seats, in great condition, you might have some trouble finding one in Denver. Although the Taurus is a popular car and Denver is a large market, the lean pickings for your choice seem a little surprising. So, for cars, eBay with its national marketplace can work magic for you (see Figure 1.1).

Figure 1.1   The home page of eBay Motors. ©1995-2004 eBay Inc.

Indeed, eBay is a perfectly logical place to buy or sell cars. If you buy a car and live within 1,000 miles of the seller, you can hop on an airplane for less than $200 and drive the car home in a weekend. If you live 3,000 miles away, you can have the car shipped for under $900. If your prospective purchase is a good deal even after factoring in the cost of delivery from a distant city and if the car is exactly what you want, why not buy it on eBay?

And, as a seller, you can potentially generate more interest in a vehicle in the national market. eBay provides a cost-effective means of reaching that market.

Indeed, eBay brings the national market to Grand Junction putting people in Grand Junction on a par with people in Denver or anywhere else.

Local Market

Even if you don't like the idea of a national market being a good place to buy or sell a used vehicle, don't forget eBay reaches local and regional markets as well.

Used Vehicles

In the 1980s, car dealers sold three new vehicles for every used vehicle sold. Today for many dealers the reverse is true. They sell three used vehicles for every new vehicle sold. The used vehicle market has become a primary business. One reason is that vehicles have become so expensive. Another reason is the higher quality of today's vehicles. They last longer, and there is less risk purchasing a used vehicle. Still another reason is that the model changes are further apart. Often you can purchase a four-year-old vehicle that looks exactly like a brand new one. The used vehicle market as a primary business looks like it's here to stay. Used vehicles can be a good deal and make a sensible purchase. (Read Chapter 3 for some numbers that show how the cost of ownership per mile of used vehicles compares to the cost of ownership per mile of new vehicles.)

Leased Vehicles

Today many people lease vehicles, typically for two or three years. Consequently, many used vehicles come off leases into the used vehicle market reasonably new and in good condition with low mileage. This fuels used vehicle sales making the used car market even more attractive.

This book is about used vehicles. Few new vehicles are sold via eBay. But today eBay is the leading national marketplace for used vehicles, a fact supported by the sales statistics cited earlier. And the used vehicle market is now the primary vehicle marketplace. In other words, your best bet on finding a vehicle that you want at a price you can afford is to shop on eBay Motors.

For Buyers and Sellers

For buyers and sellers this book:

- Fills in the details for the ideas discussed in this introduction.

- Provides you with a general working knowledge of the used-vehicle marketplace.

- Gives you the knowledge you need to be financially successful on eBay Motors.

- Assists you in protecting yourself.

- Shows you how to reduce the risk of purchasing a lemon (buyers).

- Shows you how to promote your vehicle successfully (sellers).

- Provides you with a sound basis for doing business on eBay Motors (dealers).

Indeed, we believe you can buy or sell a vehicle as safely and effectively on eBayMotors as you can locally with less trouble and less expense.

Auction?

As you will read, this book discusses negotiation between buyers and sellers quite a bit. Why is that? Aren't auctions suppose to decide the sale price? What's there to negotiate?

First, the vehicle and its price are just one part of the purchase package. In addition, there are financing, insurance, warranties, delivery, inspectons, and transaction costs that are seldom included in the auction. They are all things up for negotiation. For example, if the seller is a dealer, that dealer might provide some of the things mentioned for a negotiated price.

Second, many of the sellers on eBay Motors are dealers. Many of the transactions resulting from eBay Motors auctions, it appears, never go to the completion of an auction. Thus, everything, including the vehicle sales price, is negotiated between the buyer and the dealer.

As a consequence, this book covers dealer-buyer transactions as if they were negotiations rather than auctions. This will move many eBay members out of their eBay comfort zone. But negotiation is the reality in many transactions resulting from eBay Motors.

The Other Side of the Motors Story

Cars and trucks are the major components of the eBay motor vehicle marketplace. But they are not the only motor vehicles, and generally what we say about cars and trucks applies to other kinds of vehicles too. Boats, ATVs (all terrain vehicles), motorcycles, and RVs (recreational vehicles) all have their unique resources, but buying and selling them is not much different than buying or selling a car.

The marketplace principles are the same. For all motor vehicles a national marketplace is often better for both buyers and sellers than a local marketplace. Determining value is a prime consideration for either buying or selling. Financing is needed in many cases. Insurance is always important to motor vehicle ownership. Transportation from the seller to the buyer is often a problem in a national marketplace. Negotiation principles are the same for motor vehicles as for other items. eBay techniques are much the same whether you're selling a camera, a car, or an RV.

Perhaps the one process that differs significantly is closing a transaction. For cars, trucks, motorcycles, and RVs you have 50 different states with 50 different sets of commercial laws and 50 different licensing laws. We don't pretend to provide specific guidance to adequately cover all the states for you. Fortunately, there is a lot of similarity for such vehicles. When it comes to boats, ATVs, and other such vehicles, however, there is less similarity between the states, and it's up to you to be alert and inquire in your state as to the proper procedures and proper paperwork needed to make a transfer.

The authors don't pretend to be experts on anything except cars and trucks. But because eBay Motors encompasses other motor vehicles, Chapter 22 provides resources for obtaining information and data that will help you make good decisions whether buying or selling. Perhaps someday eBay will be so big as to warrant specialized individual books on selling boats, ATVs, motorcycles, and RVs. Until then, we believe you will do well to use this book with its focus on cars and trucks as a general guideline for your buying and selling activities on eBay for other kinds of motor vehicles.

eBay Basics

This is a specialized eBay book. It doesn't cover the eBay basics. For the basics we recommend *eBay the Smart Way* Third Edition or a similar book. To learn the basics for operating a business on eBay we recommend *eBay Business the Smart Way* or a similar book. *eBay Motors the Smart Way* assumes that you have used eBay and are confident in your basic eBay skills. Moreover, it assumes that you are confident that eBay is a safe place to buy and sell almost any type of goods including motor vehicles. If you don't yet have the necessary skills and confidence, you will probably not get the most out of this book.

eBay is not a passing fad. It is the first great institutional marketplace of the new digital age. It couldn't have—and didn't—exist before the Internet. But the Internet is here to stay. And so is eBay. Consequently, it's to your benefit to learn the basics and develop the confidence to use eBay whether it's for your everyday buying and selling activities or for buying or selling a motor vehicle.

About the Authors

The authors don't have stock in eBay nor are they employed by eBay. We are free to tell it like it is, good or bad. eBay is a fabulous new marketplace, but it has its shortcomings, and it has its hype. We are excited and enthusiastic about eBay and in particular eBay Motors. Nonetheless, we can be and are critical of eBay where appropriate, and we attempt to present an overall objective picture of eBay operations and its national marketplace.

The authors are Joseph T. Sinclair (Joe) and Don Spillane (Don). Joe has been buying cars for himself and family members for 35 years. He has practiced law, has been a commercial real estate broker and consultant, and has written books about Internet technology. He started writing his first book about eBay in 1998.

Don was a collectibles dealer in Pleasant Hill, California, and was one of eBay's biggest volume sellers in 1998. Unfortunately, after almost 30 years in business for himself, he had to move back to Connecticut in 2000 due to a family illness. He continued to operate his collectibles shop in Pleasant Hill from afar but eventually closed it.

Looking for another career, Don got into automobile sales at Acura by Executive in North Haven, Connecticut, in 2002 where he was often the top salesperson of the month. He was the first person at the dealership to sell cars on eBay, both new and used. He has sold several dozen cars on eBay thus becoming a person successful selling on eBay in two completely different industries. Recently, he became the dealership's finance manager and continues to sell cars on eBay regularly in addition to his office duties as finance manager of Acura by Executive.

Summary

So there you are. As a seller, eBay gives you an opportunity to sell for a higher price or at least make a quicker sale. As a buyer, eBay gives you an opportunity to buy at a lower price or at least choose from a larger selection. And it's a safe marketplace. What else do you need?

To take advantage of this great new marketplace, you need to develop the skills and confidence to use eBay if you have not done so already. This book will help you build on the basics to specifically buy or sell motor vehicles on eBay the smart way.

2

Used Vehicle Market

Before you can understand how to effectively and profitably buy and sell vehicles on eBay, you need to understand how the used vehicle market works offline. This chapter shows you how the cat and mouse game works between buyers and sellers (primarily dealers) offline in the real world. The online world is an extension of the offline world, and offline practices set the stage for what happens online.

To illustrate the process we will use some financially accurate examples. The numbers, however, are rounded off generic numbers and not necessarily based on specific transactions.

For Private Parties

This chapter is primarily for private parties. Dealers know this already.

Dealers

An owner goes to a dealer to buy a new car. She wants to trade in her current car for the new one. The big question is how much will the dealer give her (pay her) for her current car?

Here we have to make another assumption for analysis purposes. That is, we have to assume that the payment (trade-in allowance) for her used car has nothing to do with the remainder of the new car purchase transaction.

By giving the owner of the used vehicle a trade-in allowance, the dealer is purchasing the used car from the owner. The purchase price is the trade-in allowance.

As you will learn in Chapter 4, several publishers publish price data for new and used vehicles. Everybody uses this data. The dealers use the data, and the data is available to you free online or for a reasonable cost in printed publications.

For a certain model of a certain vehicle of a certain age with a certain mileage, the data will usually provide at least two numbers:

Wholesale value

Retail value

The wholesale number is also the trade-in value. (Sometimes the data will provide three numbers and include a number between wholesale and retail.)

For instance, a 1998 Buick LeSabre Limited with 63,000 miles in top condition was worth about $7,200 wholesale and $10,100 retail according to Edmunds in the fall of 2003.

The wholesale (trade-in) number is set by vehicle auctions. These are local auctions held regularly in which only licensed vehicle dealers can participate. Dealers sell vehicles they don't want to hold in their used car inventory, and dealers buy vehicles they want to add to their inventory.

For example, an Acura dealer might take a three-year-old Chevrolet in on trade. The dealer doesn't want Chevys on his lot. He sells high-end vehicles, and Chevys don't appeal to his customers. So, he will take the Chevy to auction. At the auction, a Chevy dealer is likely to buy the vehicle. Why? He sells a lot of used vehicles. Chevys appeal to his customers. And he can recondition (or certify) a Chevy more credibly than any other dealer.

How do the dealers bid at the auctions? They use the published price data and other factors as the basis for what they bid. The wholesale price data comes from the high bids at auctions.

The Real Trade-In Price

Ironically, the wholesale price (also called the trade-in price) is not what it says it is. Dealers have to make money just like any other business. They have huge operating overhead and personnel to pay. They cannot afford to pay you the trade-in (wholesale) price for your used vehicle and then take it to auction and sell it for the same price. They have to make a profit.

Consequently, a dealer will typically offer you $1,000 under the trade-in (wholesale) value for your car as a trade-in allowance for the new car you are buying. One way to look at it is that the dealer is charging you $1,000 to sell your used car at auction for you.

In addition, the dealer will calculate the trade-in value using data for vehicles in *fair condition*, no matter what condition the vehicle is in. This is close to the lowest possible valuation as you will learn in Chapter 4.

Is trading in your vehicle worth it? Or, should you sell the vehicle yourself? It depends. Selling a vehicle can be a time-consuming hassle. You might come out a few thousand dollars ahead selling it yourself, but for many people it's just not worth the trouble.

The Real Retail Price

The retail price is the price for which dealers sell a used vehicle. Now the Acura dealer isn't going to sell the Chevy taken in on trade. He's going to take it to auction. But if he gets a three-year-old Acura in on trade, he will keep it and sell it off his used-car lot. After all, his customers like Acuras. Will he offer it for the retail price published in the data? Probably not. He will probably offer it for more.

In any case, he will make sure the car is in the best condition possible with only a reasonable amount of money spent on reconditioning, and he will use the price data for vehicles in *excellent condition* as the basis for setting the price.

Now, the published retail price is an average price derived from the used car sales data. That means some vehicles sell above that price and some sell under that price. Consequently, although many dealers use the published retail price as a basis for determining the offering price, it doesn't mean that that's where they set the price. They often set it higher. Whether they are able to sell it at a higher price depends on the knowledge and negotiation skills of the purchaser.

Example

In this example let's look at a four-year-old high-end car with normal mileage (about 48,000 miles). The trade-in (wholesale) value is listed in the used car price data at $10,000 for a car in fair condition. A dealer will offer the owner $9,000 for the car on trade in. In other words, the dealer purchases the car for $9,000. Now the dealer owns the car and has to do something with it.

The dealer can take it to auction and make $1,000 for doing so. If the car is appropriate for the dealer's used car inventory, however, the dealer will keep the car and attempt to sell it off his used-car lot. If he does so, the price data indicates that the retail price should be $13,000 for the car in excellent condition. The dealer will probably offer the car for $14,000 or more.

The big question is, What price will the dealer actually sell the car for? That depends. If the dealer needs sales badly, he may sell the car for $10,000 to a buyer who negotiates skillfully. That's the equivalent of taking it to auction without the hassle of actually doing so. But otherwise, the dealer may elect to keep the car on the lot and hold out for a higher price. In the first 30 days, most dealers will sell this car to a buyer who can negotiate well for about $11,000.

After the car has been on the lot for over 30 days, a buyer can get a lower price. Dealers have to borrow money to finance their inventory. Thus, it cost money (interest) to hold a car in inventory. After 30 days, the dealer will start to get nervous about the car. Now the dealer has an incentive to get rid of it. A buyer who can negotiate well can probably purchase the car after 30 days for $10,000, the wholesale price.

If 90 days go by without a sale, the dealer will probably dump the car. That is, he will sell it for $9,000 (no profit). Or, he might send it to auction. At auction, however, it is now worth less than it was 90 days before, so the dealer will get only $9,500 for it.

Consequently, you can argue that the best time to purchase this car is just about the time the 90 days are up. Nonetheless, right after the car is taken in on trade is also a good time for a buyer with good negotiation skills to buy a car from a dealer who seeks a high turnover for his inventory.

Certification

The dealer will put the car (taken on trade-in) through a certification procedure (assuming it doesn't go to auction). That means that the car is checked over thoroughly, and all repairs are made so that the car is in top shape operationally. This costs a dealer from $75 to $375 plus any parts and labor needed for repairs. It is usually done for the brand of cars that the dealer sells, not necessarily for other brands.

Independent Certification

Certification is a fuzzy term. Only an Acura dealer can give an Acura an *Acura Care* certification. But any used car dealer can certify any brand of vehicle using an independent certification. For instance, Pete's Used Cars, Inc. could give any vehicle a "Super Duper Superior" certification done at a local service station.

In the earlier Acura example, there was an unstated assumption that the car was certified. If any repairs were needed, the owner of the car would have been given a lower trade-in allowance.

Acura Care certifications are based on a thorough inspection, and maintenance is brought up to date. For instance, the typical used Acura is a car coming off a lease after two or three years with about 30,000 miles. The maintenance update includes new brake pads, new front brake rotors, and new tires. This puts the Acura dealer cost of certification at the upper end of the certification cost range.

Certifications vary between different brands. They vary in scope, dealer cost, and quality. It pays to inquire what the certification means for a vehicle you are buying. It might be a good deal, or it might be of little benefit.

Are certified used cars more valuable than uncertified used cars? The pricing data shows that they generally sell for about $1,000 more. That doesn't mean a buyer has to pay $1,000 more. It costs the dealer between $75 and $375 as stated, and it's a basic service that helps the dealer sell a vehicle. So, like everything else, the value of the certification is negotiable.

Purchased Inventory

There is another scenario, however, that is commonplace. A dealer will go to auction to find used cars of the same brand he sells new in order to increase his used car inventory. He will then certify such cars. Using the same figures from the earlier example, that means the dealer will pay $10,000 at auction for an identical car. He will have to sell such a car for more than $10,000 plus the cost of certification in order to make a profit.

The benefit to the dealer is that at auction he can pick and choose his cars and buy the ones he knows will sell well. (When he takes a trade-in, it is more random and often more risky.) But in any event, he has to spend $10,000 at auction to add this car to his used car inventory.

Where does this leave the buyer? Well, the person who wants this car (obtained from the auction) may have to pay a little more to purchase it than to purchase an identical car taken on trade-in. Thus, it may help the purchaser's negotiation to find out where the car came from.

In General

Every dealer operates differently. This chapter uses a generalized example to give you an idea of how this business works. Whether buyer or seller, you have to have someplace to start in order to understand the vehicle marketplace. Although a general example like the one in this chapter may not fit your situation exactly, it's still a good place to start.

Greater Profits

Keep in mind that we're talking the fine points of the used car market. It seems like dealers sell on slim profit margins. But not every buyer is a good negotiator, so the profit margins are generally greater for dealers than is illustrated by these examples. In fact, dealers are aggressive about selling vehicles for the most money they can get, sometimes above retail value. Keep in mind, too, that the published retail value is an average indicating that dealers sell a certain percentage of used vehicles at prices greater than the published retail prices.

Non-Dealers

Private party sellers are a mixed bag. Some are knowledgeable in regard to buying and selling vehicles, and some don't have a clue as to what to do. Many believe that their vehicle is special in some way and therefore worth more. Some just want to get rid of their car at any price (I've been there myself). When you start dealing with a private party, you never know what you're getting into.

Many private parties believe they should get the full retail price for their vehicle, or more for one reason or another. This doesn't happen. Private parties can't provide some of the services and conveniences that a dealer does, and therefore their vehicles aren't worth as much. In fact, this is recognized by the general marketplace, and most private party sales prices (on the average) are somewhere between the published wholesale and retail prices.

Some publishers even publish a third price between wholesale and retail that indicates the average private party sales price. For instance, in the earlier example, a third published price might be $11,300, about halfway between the $10,000 wholesale and $13,000 retail.

The best time to buy a car from a private party is after it has been on the market for a while. There's nothing like time to make sellers more realistic about price. If a seller hasn't consulted the published price data before offering his vehicle for sale, he will eventually get around to it when the vehicle doesn't sell. Today many buyers and sellers have easy (and free) access to the used car price data on the Web. That doesn't leave a huge amount of room for negotiation. And when the negotiation is done, the agreed-upon price is often in the middle between wholesale and retail.

Strategy

What's your strategy? That, of course, depends on whether you're a buyer or seller.

Seller

A dealer's strategy is always well defined. Get as much for a car as possible but turn over the inventory as often as possible. That means that a sale with a slim profit is better than no sale.

Dealers are pros. They sell vehicles everyday and have a hundred tricks to convince buyers not only to buy but also to pay a little more than they want to pay. The buyers with good negotiation skills and appropriate background knowledge get the good deals. The other buyers pay higher prices.

If you're a private-party seller, refer to the used vehicle price data to set a realistic offering price for your vehicle. Vehicles are generally fungible. Be ready to sell at a price midway between wholesale and retail. That's where the average sale is made.

Definition

Fungible means "interchangeable" or "freely exchangeable and replaceable by another of like kind." For instance, wheat is fungible. One bag of wheat is much the same as another.

Buyer

If you're a buyer, the question is, What makes a good buyer strategy? The examples illustrate two things. First, you can get a good deal buying from a dealer if you do your homework and have good negotiation skills. Second, the deal you get from a private party depends on the private party. You might get a good deal, or you might waste a lot of time trying to negotiate an average deal. The longer a vehicle is on the market, the better your chances of the private seller reading the used car price data and getting realistic about the price.

A good strategy for buyers is to review the used vehicle price data and set a goal to purchase a vehicle at a price no more than midway between wholesale and retail. That's a goal you can realize. Sure, you can do better. But that raises another question. How long will it take to do better? Do you want to make an average deal today? Or, do you want to keep looking at vehicles for three more weeks to save $1,000?

The Numbers

Chapter 4 will show you how to get the used car data numbers and will explain more about them. But this chapter shows you how the numbers work in the market. Does buying and selling online work any differently? It does work a little differently (as discussed later in the book), but this chapter provides a basic offline overview that you will find valuable. It will help you to maximize your chances to sell at a higher price or to buy at a lower price.

Conclusion

Understanding the basics about how the used vehicle market works gives you a basis for more productive negotiations. In addition, it helps you identify situations that are to your advantage or disadvantage. After all, not all vehicles are sold at the average price. If you want to beat the average, you have to be able to spot a good deal.

3

Owning a Used Vehicle

Before you can make a wise decision as to what vehicle you buy, you need to evaluate the overall picture. That includes a variety of considerations, most of which we can't help you with. However, we can help you evaluate the financial aspects of owning your next vehicle.

Let's take a look at some factors you need to consider in purchasing a vehicle:

Utility Decide what you need before you buy.

Safety This is a matter requiring research and is certainly worthy of your time and attention.

Emotion You need to be comfortable with the image conveyed by the vehicle you buy.

Finance When you figure out the real cost of owning a vehicle, it may help you make a better decision.

This chapter briefly covers the first three and spends the remainder of the chapter on the fourth, finance.

Utility

If you're single and fancy free, a two-seat sports car may be all you need. If you're married with three kids, a mini-van might be your best bet. If you need to move a lot of stuff around all the time, a pickup truck may make your life easier. If you live in snow country, an SUV with four-wheel drive will help keep you moving in the winter.

The problem is that buying a car is often an impulse buy. It's summer and buying a convertible seems the obvious thing to do. But then winter comes, and you wonder what you were thinking last summer when you made the purchase. Or, it's summer and you buy an SUV looking ahead to the winter when four-wheel drive will provide you with more dependable transportation in the snow. But winter comes and you discover that you've bought an SUV without four-wheel drive, leaving you with a rear-wheel-drive vehicle no better than the least snow-worthy car.

You need to put some thought into what you need. Then you need to put some research into which vehicles are going to give you what you need. It's always a trade-off. Few vehicles will give you everything you need. But deciding what you're going to buy before you make your purchase will help you make a more satisfying purchase decision.

Here are some resources that will help you find a vehicle that meets your needs:

AutoTrader Features a useful used car research system, which enables you find comprehensive information on models as old as 1983. See *http://www.autotrader.com*.

Edmunds Provides consumer ratings and reviews as well as editors' reviews for used cars. See *http://www.edmunds.com*.

Safety

Some cars are supposedly safer than others, and many people put a lot of importance on safety reports. But common sense is a factor here too. The safest little car is going to come out on the short end in a collision with the least safe full-size pickup truck. Our advice is to spend time doing enough research on safety to satisfy yourself that you can make a reasonable decision. Here are some resources:

Consumer Reports Used Car Buying Guide, Consumers Union, New York (annual).

AutoTrader Through its used car research system it includes safety information and specifications. See *http://www.autotrader.com*.

National Highway Traffic Safety Administration Provides a wealth of information on vehicle safety. See *http://www.nhtsa.dot.gov*.

Emotion

Vehicles are often tied to our image of ourselves. If you're a soccer mom or dad, you're probably going to feel comfortable with a minivan. You might not feel comfortable with a two-seat sports car, which enables you to chauffer around only one child. The other parents might wonder what you're trying to prove, and peer pressure will start to change your image of yourself.

Emotion also has to do with what you *want* in contrast to what you *need*. Another way of putting this is that image indicates what you need emotionally in contrast to what you need in regard to a vehicle's operational utility.

The image-vehicle connection is one for a team of psychiatrists to unravel, and we're not going to touch it. But it's not a factor you should ignore. You need to balance your wants with your needs to make a satisfying decision. The best way to do so is to think it through ahead of time before you go looking for your next vehicle.

Finance

You can accurately determine the cost of owning a vehicle if you take all the relevant expenses into consideration. This can be an eye-opening exercise and may have a major impact on your purchasing decision. And this book can help with this particualr consideration.

The Exercise

In this section we will look at the purchase of a new luxury car to determine the cost of ownership for four years and eight years. Then we will look at the purchase of the same vehicle as a four-year-old used car to determine the cost of ownership for the second four years.

Next we will do the same analysis for a mid-priced vehicle to compare the cost of ownership.

This is based on the following assumptions, which may or may not match your experience or requirements:

1. The example vehicles will be driven 12,000 miles per year.

2. They will have 48,000 miles on the odometer at the end of the fourth year and 96,000 at the end of the eighth year.

3. Repairs in the first four years will be nominal. Repairs in the second four years will be low.

The reason longer ownership periods are not used in this chapter is because there is a general expectation that vehicles over 100,000 miles begin to require major repairs, and many people will sell to avoid owning a car with over 100,000 miles.

Over 100,000 Miles

If you typically own vehicles with over 100,000 miles, you can still do an analysis. Just be realistic about the higher repair costs.

For your analysis, you need to use figures with which you are comfortable. Not all vehicles are the same. Not all usage is the same. Not all ownership periods are the same. Not all drivers drive the same. Not all vehicles are of the same durability.

It's not important to have precise figures when you do this analysis. This is not an accounting exercise. Use the most accurate estimates you can find through research or from your own experience. They will give you a reasonably accurate idea of what you will spend over your ownership period.

The Vehicles

The first vehicle is an actual 1999 Lincoln Town Car, which Joe bought in 2003. This is a luxury car that comes with just about every option. It costs an expensive $37,000 new (about 10 percent below sticker). This four-year-old car had a wholesale value of $13,847 with 48,000 miles on the odometer. It was in perfect condition. Joe found it on eBay in a city only a one-day drive from home. It was Joe's goal to buy it at the wholesale price. (Joe actually bought it below the wholesale price, but the wholesale price is used below in the expense analysis.)

The second vehicle is a less expensive mid-size Mercury Sable, a comparison vehicle.

The Expenses Worksheet

The vehicle expenses worksheet contains straightforward numbers, but it may contain some that you would otherwise forget to include were you not to use this worksheet:

Purchase Price

Sales Taxes

Delivery Expenses (for buying on eBay)

Total

Sales Price (at the end of ownership)

Depreciation (x miles)

Depreciation

Financing Expense (interest)

License Fees

Insurance

Gas

Maintenance

Repairs

Total Expenses

Cost/Mile

Let's take a look at how these numbers work for two different vehicles.

New Town Car (96,000)

These numbers reflect the ownership of a new Lincoln Town Car for a period of eight years and 96,000 miles.

Purchase Price $37,633

Sales Taxes $3,010

Delivery Expenses *None*

Total $40,643

Sales Price $5,460

Depreciation (96,000 miles) $35,183

Depreciation $35,183

Financing Expense $4,790

License Fees $3,000

Insurance $5,200

Gas $8,470

Maintenance $4,000

Repairs $1,500

Total Expenses $62,143

Cost/Mile $0.65

New Town Car (48,000)

These numbers reflect the ownership of a new Lincoln Town Car for a period of four years and 48,000 miles.

Purchase Price $37,633

Sales Taxes $3,010

Delivery Expenses *None*

Total $40,643

Sales Price $13,847

Depreciation (48,000 miles) $26,796

Depreciation $26,796

Financing Expense $4,790

License Fees $1,000

Insurance $2,600

Gas $4,235

Maintenance $2,000

Repairs $1,000

Total Expenses $42,421

Cost/Mile $0.88

Used Town Car

These numbers reflect the ownership of a four-year-old used Lincoln Town Car for a second four-year period and 48,000 additional miles.

Purchase Price $13,847

Sales Taxes $1,107

Delivery Expenses $500

Total $15,454

Sales Price $5,460

Depreciation (48,000 miles) $9,994

Depreciation $9,994

Financing Expense $1,762

License Fees $1,000

Insurance $2,600

Gas $4,235

Maintenance $2,000

Repairs $1,000

Total Expenses $22,591

Cost/Mile $0.47

New Sable (96,000)

These numbers reflect the ownership of a new Mercury Sable for a period of eight years and 96,000 miles.

Purchase Price $19,435

Sales Taxes $1,554

Delivery Expenses *None*

Total $20,989

Sales Price $3,124

Depreciation (96,000 miles) $17,865

Depreciation $17,865

Financing Expense $2,473

License Fees $2,000

Insurance $5,200

Gas $6,545

Maintenance $4,000

Repairs $1,500

Total Expenses $39,583

Cost/Mile $0.41

New Sable (48,000)

These numbers reflect the ownership of a new Mercury Sable for a period of four years and 48,000 miles.

Purchase Price $19,435

Sales Taxes $1,554

Delivery Expenses *None*

Total $20,989

Sales Price $7,241

Depreciation (48,000 miles) $13,748

Depreciation $13,748

Financing Expense $2,473

License Fees $600

Insurance $2,600

Gas $3,272

Maintenance $2,000

Repairs $1,000

Total Expenses $25,693

Cost/Mile $0.54

Used Sable

These numbers reflect the ownership of a used four-year-old Mercury Sable for a second four-year period and 48,000 additional miles.

Purchase Price $7,241

Sales Taxes $579

Delivery Expenses $500

Total $8,320

Sales Price $3,124

Depreciation (48,000 miles) $5,196

Depreciation $5,196

Financing Expense $921

License Fees $600

Insurance $2,600

Gas $3,272

Maintenance $2,000

Repairs $1,000

Total Expenses $15,589

Cost/Mile $0.32

The Numbers Explained

This subsection will give you a better idea of the origin of the numbers so you can easily duplicate the worksheet.

Purchase Price

For new car purchase prices, we used the sticker price less 10 percent, which reflects a normal discount given to those who negotiate.

For the used car purchase prices we used the Private Party price from Edmunds (see Chapter 4).

(For leased vehicles see the sidebar Leased Vehicles in the subsection Financing Expenses.)

Sales Taxes

For sales tax we used 8 percent of the purchase price. This will vary from state to state, and five states do not even have sales tax. You pay the sales tax in your own state when you register the vehicle regardless of where you bought it.

You are usually charged some small fees in the state where you purchase the vehicle.

Delivery Expenses

Normally, you would purchase locally and take delivery for no expense. However, on eBay Motors, 75 percent of the purchases take place across state lines. Consequently, your delivery expenses might include transportation, motel, and food; that is, you might have to fly 1,000 miles and drive the vehicle home. Or, you might decide to have the vehicle shipped home.

We did not enter a delivery cost for the vehicles bought new, because new vehicles are not widely sold on eBay.

The Miles Count Too

As you will see, it's more expensive to drive a car home than you think. We did not include the cost of the miles driving home in the delivery expense. If you do, it may be a considerable extra expense. You will find that in many cases having the car shipped home makes more financial sense than traveling to drive it home yourself.

Sales Price

We estimated the sales prices (for used vehicles) using the Edmunds Private Party price under the assumption that you will sell it yourself. Use the Edmunds Trade-In price less $1,000 if you will trade it in on another vehicle at the end of the ownership period.

(For leased vehicles see the sidebar Leased Vehicles in the subsection Financing Expenses.)

Depreciation

The depreciation expense is: Purchase Price + Sales Taxes + Delivery Expenses − Sales Price = Depreciation. You pay the depreciation up front if you pay cash. However, if you get a loan, you pay the depreciation, in effect, as you make installment payments on the loan. In any event, depreciation is a major expense.

Financing Expense

The financing expense is the amount of interest you pay over the life of the vehicle loan until it's paid off. A loan officer can figure that out for you. (See Chapter 6 to find out how to easily calculate the interest expense on a loan yourself.) We used a 4-year amortization at 6 percent for the loan, and we assumed that the loan was equal to the purchase price (not including sales tax).

Leased Vehicles

For a leased vehicle, the purchase price is 0, and the sales price is 0. Most leases are made at full price, and the vehicle goes back to the leasing company at the end of the lease. The lease payments include the financing expense and all of the depreciation including sales tax (unless sales tax was paid separately at the beginning of the lease). Therefore, the figure to enter for financing expense is the total of the lease payments.

We don't include lease calculations examples in this chapter because this book is primarily about used vehicles, and used vehicles are not normally leased. Nonetheless, many dealers now have used vehicle leasing programs.

License Fees

The license fee is the annual fee to license the vehicle times the number of years of ownership. This is a nominal amount in some states and a substantial amount in others.

Insurance

This is the annual insurance cost for adequate coverage times the number of years of ownership. This depends on many factors, and you will need to get an estimate from your insurance agent.

Gas

The fuel expense depends on the gas mileage for the vehicle and the price of gas. Calculate it for the period of ownership. The formula is: miles ÷ miles/gallon × the price/gallon.

Example: 48,000 miles ÷ 17 miles per gallon × $1.50 per gallon = $4,235

Maintenance

This includes expenses such as oil changes, air filters, windshield wipers, brake pads, coolant, belts, hoses, special fluids, tires, and the like. The vehicle owner's manual will provide a schedule for maintenance, which you can use to make estimates. We used $2,000 for each 48,000 miles for both vehicles.

Note that this figure will be higher if a dealer does the maintenance. A competent local mechanic can do most maintenance on almost any vehicle and will usually charge less than a dealer's service department. Good maintenance does not necessarily require a dealer.

Repairs

This is an arbitrary amount, which you should base on your own experience. We used $500 for the first 48,000 miles and $1,000 for the second 48,000 miles for both vehicles. Obviously this would not cover a lemon or anything close to a lemon. And clearly after 96,000 miles this cost will escalate considerably for most vehicles. Nonetheless, vehicles last longer today, and it's not unreasonable to expect a well-maintained vehicle to go 100,000 without a major repair.

Note again that this figure will be higher if a dealer does the repairs. A competent local mechanic can do most routine repairs on almost any vehicle and will usually charge less than a dealer's service department. There is a huge after-market industry providing high-quality parts for routine repairs, and a local mechanic can also get manufacturer's parts when required for uncommon repairs. Repairs do not necessarily require a dealer.

Of course, if you don't know a competent local independent mechanic—and they are difficult to find—taking your Chevy to a Chevy dealer for maintenance and repairs is your bet bet.

Total Expenses

This is a total of all the expenses including depreciation. The formula is: Depreciation + Financing Expense + License Fees + Insurance + Gas + Maintenance + Repairs = Total Expenses.

Cost Per Mile

This is the Total Expenses divided by the number of miles driven during the ownership period.

Example: $22,769 total expenses ÷ 48,000 miles = $0.47 per mile.

The Cost Per Mile

The cost per mile is the figure! It enables you to easily compare one vehicle, new or used, to another and make a sound financial decision. If one vehicle costs 22 cents per mile and another costs 26 cents per mile, you can eyeball roughly a 20 percent difference (actually a 18.2 percent difference). Is the second vehicle worth 20 percent more? In fact, in many cases the second vehicle may have a lower purchase price but nonetheless a higher per-mile cost.

But what's a 20 percent difference when it comes to buying a vehicle? It's probably not a big deal unless you're on a tight budget. But what about an 80 percent difference? At some point the numbers tell you that one vehicle is a good deal for you and another is not.

Let's look at the six ownership examples in this chapter to compare them in Table 3.1.

Table 3.1 Ownership Calculations

	New 0 to 48,000	New 0 to 96,000	Used 48,000 to 96,000
Town Car	$0.88	$0.65	$0.47
Sable	$0.54	$0.41	$0.32

You can see that the first person to own the Town Car paid almost twice as much per mile as the second owner who drove it the second 48,000 miles. The four-year-old used Town Car cost less to own than a new Sable driven for 48,000 miles but more to own than a new Sable driven for 96,000 miles.

Leased Vehicles

Calculations show that the new Sable owned for the first 48,000 on a lease would cost $0.61 per mile instead of $0.54 per mile for normal ownership with a loan. Lease payments are lower than loan payments, but overall it costs more to own a leased vehicle than a normally financed one.

This analysis does not take into consideration using a leased vehicle in a business where certain income tax advantages may change the cost analysis.

Comparisons like this can help you make decisions. The used Town Car cost only 42 percent more to own than the used Sable but had a purchase price 91 percent higher. Thus, Joe concluded that owning a used Town Car was a pretty good deal even though it had a higher price than the used Sable. However, Joe wouldn't have bought a brand new Town Car.

Don't Argue

Don't argue with us about our figures. Use your own figures instead. The point to this chapter is not what figures are more accurate, but rather to use the form provided so that you don't leave out any expenses.

If you don't want to use your own figures, there is statistical data published. For statistics on the operational costs of various vehicles try the AAA Missouri website (*http://www.aaamissouri.com/news/library/drivingcost*). Their data shows that a new Chevorlet Cavlier LS (medium car) costs about $0.44 mile; a new Ford Taurus SEL (large car) costs about $0.51 per mile; and a new Mercury Grand Marquis LS (luxury car) costs about $0.59 per mile. This data is based on driving 15,000 miles per year.

Used Vehicles

The examples used in this chapter are not haphazard. They are intended to show that it makes financial sense to buy used vehicles. Keep in mind that the used cars evaluated here were all in perfect condition. Realistically, few used vehicles are in perfect condition, but most with low mileage are in pretty good condition and can be put in near perfect condition with little expense. The fact is that used vehicles can be a good deal.

Over 100,000 Miles

Even when you consider owning a car with over 100,000 miles, buying a used car makes sense. Although a vehicle with over 100,000 is more prone to major repairs, owning one and paying for major repairs can be considerably less expensive than buying a new vehicle. The first owner of every new vehicle takes a huge depreciation hit. That amount of money can pay for several major repairs. See Chapter 5 for more information on the risk of repairs.

As for Joe's experience, he bought the Lincoln Town Car (see Figure 3.1) with 49,800 miles for $11,250 on eBay (under wholesale). It cost about $160 and two days to take the train to the distant city (no major airport), spend the night in a motel, and drive back home. Nice car! Good price!

Figure 3.1   1999 Lincoln Town Car.

Author's Requirements

Joe's family already had an SUV and didn't want another SUV or van. But his daughter had just started driving, and he wanted a large heavy car that would hold its own in an accident. It was also important to have six seats to ferry as many high school kids around as possible. The choice narrowed to a hand full of big cars. They all fell in a narrow price range. Why not buy the most luxurious or the best deal? In this case, the most luxurious turned out to be the best deal too. Needless to say, Joe's teenage daughter doesn't like this car, but at least she'll be safer. As for Joe, he's enjoying the prestige of ownership, even if it is pre-owned prestige.

Test Drive

Is eBay the first or last resort? It's never first. Decide what you will buy. If you can go to your local auto mall or visit several local dealers and find a vehicle that suits your requirements at a price you have targeted, why go anywhere else? There are better things to do with your life than look at cars forever. Why buy a vehicle in another city where you have to take time off to travel if you can get the same deal at home?

Shopping locally solves two issues. First, you can get a good idea of whether you can easily find a vehicle locally. If so, do some more local shopping. If not, don't keep looking. Go to eBay.

Second, it gives you a chance to test drive the vehicles that fit your requirements, even if the vehicles don't fit exactly. For instance, suppose you're looking for a three-year-old Buick Century with no more than 36,000 miles. You find one that has 60,000 miles. It isn't a fit, but test drive it anyway. With a test drive, you may find that you don't really like the Buick Century, and you wouldn't buy one at any price. Or, perhaps you find that a Buick Century drives even better than you thought, and it might not be so bad to buy one even with high mileage. You can't test drive a vehicle on eBay.

Vehicles have so many variables (brand, model, color, options, condition, mileage, price, etc.) that perhaps you won't find what you're looking for locally. But at least by shopping locally you will be able to test drive some of the models of your choice.

Authors' Choice

We believe that how a vehicle drives is very important to almost everyone. It's certainly important to us. Let's say it falls under Utility. Test driving the individual vehicle that you buy on eBay is not feasible until you travel to the seller's city to complete the purchase. But test driving the identical model locally is something you should do well before you resort to shopping on eBay.

Summary

It pays to think ahead before you buy a vehicle. Think through utility, safety, and emotion. Run the numbers to get an accurate financial picture. Then make a decision as to what you will look for. Shop locally. Do some test drives. Finally, if you can't find a good deal locally, proceed to eBay where you will find the largest selection of used vehicles available anywhere.

II

Personal Buying

4

Prices

The one best technique—and experts are in unanimous agreement on this—for auctioning an item or bidding on an item is to know the value. Indeed, that holds true for negotiation too. Fortunately for cars and trucks, knowing the value is easy to master with a little research. The data is available on the Web and in numerous publications.

If you don't know the value of the vehicle you are buying or selling, you are at a tremendous disadvantage, because you can bet that the other party does. So, take the time to do your homework, and you will come out thousands of dollars ahead.

On the Web

The vehicle price data publishers have websites where you can look up the market value (price) of both new and used cars and trucks. Such websites are easy to use, and the price data is dependably accurate.

Edmunds

For many years we have been buying Edmunds vehicle price booklets purchased from bookstores. Edmunds price booklets for a long time were the only price booklets you could consistently find in bookstores around the US. They appeared every quarter. Now Edmunds is on the Web with a valuable site at *http://www.edmunds.com* (see Figure 4.1).

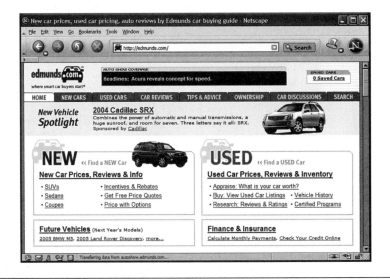

Figure 4.1   Edmunds website. ©1995-2004 Edmunds.com Inc.

You can estimate the value of new and used vehicles free at the Edmunds website. It's quick and easy to do. It gives you options for fine tuning your appraisals. We find it very useful.

Kelley Blue Book

Although the Kelley Blue Book has not been as easily available to the general public as Edmunds, it has been a favorite among dealers and bankers, particularly on the West Coast. Indeed it has given the generic name to price booklets: blue book. Many people use the term "blue book" to refer to price booklets in general whether for vehicles or even for other types of equipment.

Kelley has a useful website (*http://www.kbb.com*) at which for no cost you can easily estimate the value of new and used vehicles quickly (see Figure 4.2).

Figure 4.2   Kelley's website. ©2004 Kelley Blue Book.

(It also provides pricing for motorcycles, ATVs, personal watercraft, and snowmobiles. See chapter 22.)

NADA

These price booklets are used by dealers and bankers and are available to the public in some bookstores now. NADA (National Automobile Dealers Association) has a website (*http://www.nada.com*) where you can go to estimate the value of new and used vehicles for free (see Figure 4.3).

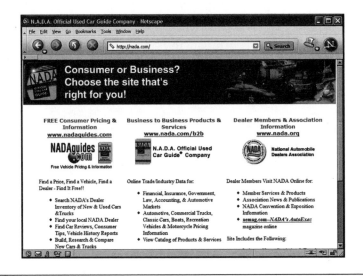

Figure 4.3   NADA website.

(It also provides pricing for classic cars, motorcyles, snowmobiles, ATVs, personal watercraft, power boats, sailboats, RVs, and aircraft. See chapter 22.)

Galves

This subscription service is used by dealers, particularly on the East Coast. Galves also has a website (*http://www.galves.com*) where you can get vehicle prices. The website pricing service is available only by subscription.

Black Book

This subscription service is used primarily by dealers in the South. It has a website (*http://www.blackbookusa.com*) where subscribers can get vehicle prices.

Variances

These price guides don't coincide exactly. Edmunds assumes the average annual mileage to be 12,000 miles, and penalizes vehicles with mileage above that. NADA assumes the average annual mileage to be 12,500 to 13,000 and penalizes mileage above that. The Kelley Blue Book assumes the average annual mileage to be 13,000 miles and penalizes mileage above that. Thus, Kelley prices are the highest, presumably because Kelley allows the highest average annual mileage.

Galves (available by subscription only) assumes the average mileage to be about 11,500 annually.

Comparisons

The table below shows the fall 2003 pricing for a 1999 Buick Park Avenue with 65,000 miles (13,000 miles annually). Note that such a vehicle is considered to be five years old. See Table 4.1.

Table 4.1 Ownership Calculations

	Trade-In	Private Party	Retail
Galves	$7,300	NA	NA
Edmunds	$8,535	$9,954	$11,472
NADA	$9,275	NA	$11,550
Kelley Blue Book	$9,850	$11,725	$13,635

If you adjust the prices for the differences in the annual mileage allowances, they are a little closer. Nonetheless the differences remain considerable between pricing guides.

The Galves-Kelley variance (substantial) is partially explained by the East-West Coast difference mentioned below in the *Regional Differences* subsection. The Galves price was not keyed to a ZIP code. All the other prices were calculated with a West Coast ZIP code. When the Kelley Trade-In price is recalculated with an East Coast ZIP code, the value is $9,075, which is $775 less than the West Coast price.

Don explains that the Galves prices are a true dealers' trade-in values; that is, around $1,000 below the local auctions. The other trade-in (wholesale) prices are based on auction price statistics.

We have not done a study to determine the discrepancies for the four services on all vehicles. However, we invite you to run the numbers for your vehicle on three services (available free) just to get an accurate picture of the price ranges.

Confused? That's understandable. It's seems as if the pricing services, if accurate, would be more uniform. But they are not. We have found Edmunds to be very useful and accurate in buying and selling vehicles over the years. But the one you find to be the most accurate, may be the one you use the most—a kind of self-fulfilling prophesy.

Dual Use

You will find dealers who use dual pricing services. For instance, the dealer will give the owner of the Park Avenue a $7,200 (Galves) trade-in allowance and then turn around and sell it on his lot for $13,635 (Kelley). He can claim published prices for each pricing.

Regional Differences

You use a ZIP code to key the price services. There are likely to be regional differences. For instance, a vehicle on the East Coast is likely to be priced lower than the same vehicle on the West Coast. Why? Vehicles are in better shape in the West due to the arid environment (e.g., no rust). Also, certain models may be more popular (and command a premium price) in one part of the country than another.

Consequently, when negotiating, you might want to use the value in the region where you are buying. In deciding the value to yourself, however, you might want to use the value in your home region.

Many dealers will tell you that the pricing services are not accurate, that you can better estimate values by knowing the local market, and that local price research will pay off. All of that is true, and that's why it's important to shop locally before you buy on eBay. In the end, though, you will need to rely on the pricing services to give you an idea of what the price range is. You can't take the time to become a true expert on the local market.

Others rely on the pricing services. Why not you? What else can you do? Buying and selling vehicles is not an exact science, and relying on pricing services sure beats operating in the dark.

The Spread

What does the spread between wholesale and retail value mean? The dealer sells the vehicle traded in (or purchased at auction) for a markup to cover expenses and make a profit. A dealer's expenses include the following:

- Advertising
- Dealership overhead
- Financing to carry inventory
- Preparation of vehicles for sale
- Salesperson's commission

A private sale is not the same. The seller in a private sale has lower expenses than a dealer. Then too, such a seller cannot provide the services that a dealer can provide. That's the reason that private sales tend to have a purchase price between wholesale value and retail value, often closer to wholesale.

Get Organized

The valuable price data you can get on the websites above won't do you much good unless you use it in an organized and systematic way.

Develop a procedure for buying a vehicle. Look. Gather information. Take the time to do price research. And then bid or negotiate. Impulse buying is a strong force in the vehicle market. Don't let your impulses prevent you from taking the time to gather all the facts and to do your research.

A typical seller has a fantasy about the value of his vehicle. Somehow it's worth a few thousand more than the published data indicates. But the typical seller uses the same data as the buyers. How can they get a higher price?

In a few cases, it might be ignorance, but in many cases it's just plain subjectivity. The seller perceives the vehicle to be in prime condition when it's really in good condition with a few noticeable defects. The seller perceives the vehicle to have valuable optional equipment that somehow is not listed in the market data. But such options have little or no value. The seller perceives the vehicle to be rare and popular when actually it's rare because it never sold well. And so on.

Sellers can be quite adamant about the value of their vehicles citing the same data sources that buyers are using but coming up with different figures. What's the best defense to the unrealistic seller? Well-researched market data from Edmunds, Kelley, or NADA is the best defense. If you're a buyer and know your pricing data, you will have the confidence to negotiate strongly and persistently and to stand up to misguided sellers. Otherwise, you're at a disadvantage that may be difficult to overcome.

If you're a seller, avoid being subjective. Otherwise you will price your vehicle out of the market and waste your time trying to sell it. Go by the book and use prices properly calculated.

And always attempt to find out what pricing service the other party is using. This will give you more background knowledge to use in your negotiations.

The Last Stop

After you've priced a vehicle by careful research via the pricing services, there's one last stop to make in order to adjust your price if appropriate. That's eBay itself. eBay archives at least three weeks of completed auctions. The completed auctions are a good place to go to find out what popular models are selling for on eBay. (The data for non-popular models will probably not be conclusive.) It could be that the archived auctions are out of sync with the pricing services. If the eBay prices are too high, you will probably go elsewhere to find a vehicle. If they're low, eBay may present a real opportunity for you to make a steal. The archives are a good place for you to end your pricing research and get on with the business of bidding.

Note that eBay now sells price data to affluent retailers and other affluent businesses for a wide range of items. (The word "affluent" means that only those with deep pockets can afford to purchase the data.) For many items, eBay is the definitive price-setting market now. Nonetheless, the vehicle pricing services discussed above still use more complete data than can be derived from eBay Motors.

Andale Pricing

Andale, an auction management service, provides an appraisal service based on eBay sales data. You can subscribe for $3 per month.

Purchase Price

Purchase negotiations need to be realistic to be successful. As a buyer, your first step in negotiating a transaction is to determine the values for a particular vehicle. Our experience over the years shows the following for the final purchase price (based on Edmunds):

Above Retail You've been conned.

At Retail You've made an average purchase. Nothing wrong with that if purchased from a dealer.

Between Retail and Wholesale You've made a good buy.

At Wholesale You've made a great buy.

Below Wholesale You've made a steal. You are in danger of being arrested.

In regard to eBay, you have to shift down a little to take into account the cost of delivery:

Above Retail You've paid much too much.

At Retail You've paid too much.

Between Retail and Wholesale You've made an average purchase.

At Wholesale You've made a good buy.

Below Wholesale You've made a great buy.

Why are vehicles less valuable on eBay? There are two reasons. First, the sales effort is potentially less trouble and less expensive for the seller; therefore he or she can accept a lower price. Second, a buyer takes more risk buying a car in a faraway place than he or she does locally. Therefore, buyers are not willing to pay quite as much for vehicles on eBay as they would locally. Buyers also have the expense of getting the vehicle home.

How should you bid? You need to determine the top price you're willing to spend for a particular vehicle and then bid up to it. In other words, bid it just like any other auction using published values to guide you.

Not Due to Skill

Joe's purchase of the Lincoln Town Car at about $2,500 under wholesale wasn't due to skillful purchasing. He just happen to be in the right place at the right time, so to speak. In other words, he got lucky. Perhaps you will get lucky on eBay too. But you can't count on it. If you can buy the vehicle you want at a price midway between wholesale and retail less your delivery cost, you're doing just fine—and better than most other buyers.

Determining a Vehicle's eBay Value

Read the earlier section in this chapter on determining value. If you realistically want to sell your vehicle on eBay, you will need to sell it at a price that appeals to eBay buyers. It's not likely that you will sell it at full retail value for the following three reasons:

1. In the local market you will have a difficult time selling a vehicle at full retail value. A typical private sale (not a dealer sale) in our experience is closer to wholesale than to retail value.

2. A normal eBay buyer has to spend $200–$900 to pick up the vehicle or have it delivered. That has to come out of the price, or what's the point of buying on eBay?

3. A buyer runs the risk of traveling to pick up the vehicle in a distant city, being dissatisfied with the misrepresented condition of the vehicle, and returning home empty-handed. That could cost as much as $500 or more, a substantial risk. It's not smart to take that risk and pay full retail too.

As a seller you might ask, What's the point of trying to sell a vehicle on eBay if sales prices are likely to be lower than full retail? There are several answers to that question:

1. A local sale is likely to be lower than full retail too.

2. A $200–$900 downward price adjustment looks less significant as the price of the vehicle increases.

3. Some vehicles will take a long time to sell in the local market, perhaps many months. It may be quicker to find a buyer on eBay.

4. For many vehicles, there are more potential buyers on eBay than locally. That means more possibilities and a greater likelihood of a successful transaction.

5. If you sell only via eBay, you are not likely to have a lot of people coming to your home to take a look at the vehicle.

6. Selling on eBay is easier than selling locally in many cases.

7. There are always potential eBay buyers who live in your city. Thus, an eBay auction has local possibilities.

Summary

Experts agree. Accurate pricing is the key to successful buying and selling on eBay, particularly for vehicles. There is free information online readily available on vehicle valuation. Use it to your advantage. Make it a routine part of your buying or selling procedure to check the price of each vehicle. Be sure to use accurate information on every vehicle that you price to ensure the pricing process generates an accurate valuation.

And by the way, pricing vehicles accurately is also a good strategy for negotiation, which Chapter 16 covers, and for other vehicles and marketplaces, which Chapters 22 and 23 cover.

5

Quality Checks

How do you protect yourself against purchasing a defective vehicle? Well, you do it much the same on eBay as you do for a local purchase. The difference is that you can learn to do it better via eBay. Indeed, eBay makes all the tools handy and also reasonably inexpensive.

Inspections

Physical inspections are one of the best means of evaluating a potential purchase. The inspection of records is also important for what it might reveal about a vehicle's history.

A Local Purchase

The standard buying procedure is to visually inspect a vehicle. In other words, take a good look at it. You can judge the exterior and interior condition reasonably accurately yourself. Driving the vehicle, of course, is important. Always take a test drive. But it's the engine that requires some expertise. Always take the vehicle to a mechanic who does inspections for car purchases. Such inspections cost $50–$100.

Don't deal with a seller who will not let you take the vehicle for an inspection by a mechanic. Take a pass and find another vehicle to buy. Otherwise you take the risk that the engine (or some other major component) is malfunctioning.

From your visual inspection, a test drive, and a mechanic's inspection, you will get a pretty accurate idea of the true condition of the vehicle. This procedure is not foolproof, but it's obviously much better than ignoring the risk.

eBay Purchase

Alas, when you buy a vehicle on eBay in a distant city, what can you do? First, deal only with eBay sellers who have good reputations (solid positive feedback). Second, get full information on the vehicle. Third, look at plenty of photographs, one from every angle, to do a preliminary visual inspection. Fourth, if the seller did not include photographs in the auction ad, request them. If the seller doesn't provide them, forget that vehicle and move on to another.

Based on honest information from a reputable seller, you can make a reasonably safe decision. Certainly, it's not a risk-free decision, but it's workable. Bear in mind, if the vehicle turns out to be as represented, you're stuck buying it. You better test drive one exactly like it locally before you commit yourself to some heavy bidding.

Should you arrive in the distant city to find the vehicle is not as represented, you have reasonable grounds to back out of the deal, and you should do so. Accordingly, you should, if possible, travel to the distant city to inspect the vehicle immediately after the auction and before the seller requires you to put down a deposit. Otherwise, in a dispute, you may lose your deposit.

Your Inspection

Use your common sense when you inspect the vehicle. If something looks askew, it may indicate a defective or damaged vehicle. If you see paint on rubber gaskets, it means that the vehicle has been painted since it left the factory. Run your finger along the inside edges of the fenders, hood, and trunk. If you feel a slight ridge, it may be a ridge caused by the masking tape used during the repainting process. They don't use masking tape at the factories. Paint discrepancies may mean the vehicle has been in an accident.

If a vehicle has damage, however slight, don't assume it will be inexpensive to repair. Unless you're an expert, you will be surprised how expensive some repairs can be that seem minor. And contrarily, some defects that seem major are easily repaired with an inexpensive replacement part. Ask questions. If necessary, bring in (or go to) a third party expert (e.g., a body shop) to get an evaluation.

Test Drive and Engine Inspection

It's the seller's choice whether to allow you a test drive or perform an engine inspection after the end of the auction and before completing the transaction. Because these inspections are your best protection against getting a lemon, it seems silly to travel all the way to the seller's city to pick up the vehicle if the seller won't let you (an out-of-towner) do what most sellers will allow buyers in their locale to do. An honest seller takes little risk in permitting these inspections. After all, it's the buyer who travels at her own expense to make these inspections. It takes a serious buyer to do so. Therefore, if these inspections aren't allowed, take a pass and go on to another vehicle.

Interestingly, a test drive and inspection before you make payment is also your best defense against fraud. Don't bypass this part of the purchase process.

Before the Auction?

Some sellers allow an inspection and test drive only before the end of the auction but not after. This doesn't make sense. This is not workable for out-of-town buyers.

Chief Mechanic Victor Owens of Brooks Automotive, who has taken good care of Joe's family cars for many years, recommends the following:

- Ask for a pre-purchase check. This is similar to one normally done during an oil change and lubrication, except more thorough. Check to see that everything on the vehicle, both inside and outside, works.

- Ask for a smog check (required upon transfer in some states). This is not cost-effective unless the seller is in the same state as the buyer. However, a successful smog check generally indicates that a vehicle operates properly, but it is not conclusive.

- When a vehicle has over 80,000 miles, have each engine cylinder's compression checked manually. A compression check done on a scope saves time and sometimes costs less, but it is not as accurate as a manual check.

- Make sure the vehicle is checked in daylight, not at night.

- Ask the mechanic do a test drive. In a test drive, a mechanic can uncover problems that others would miss.

For older vehicles especially, the most important test is for cylinder compression. If the engine passes the cylinder compression test, it will probably not require major repair work soon.

Compression Check

Joe was buying a car for his mother once in the 1990s. It was a two-year-old Ford with 19,000 miles. He had a mechanic run a compression check, which turned out negative. The mechanic double checked. The engine had a serious loss of compression in two cylinders. Joe returned it to the used car dealer who refused to believe it, or said he refused to believe it. However, there was another identical Ford also available, which Joe took for a check with the same mechanic. This one checked out fine, and his mother bought it. The first check undoubtedly adverted a very premature engine overhaul.

Although Mr. Owens recommends a compression check only for vehicles over 80,000 miles, at the slightest hint of poor engine performance, you will do well to include a compression check at any mileage. For instance, if the engine knocks, misfires, or doesn't run smoothly, it's obviously a sign that the engine needs at least a tune up. But it might be a sign that the engine needs more. Run a compression check just to be sure.

Inspections don't necessarily take a long time, but scheduling is sometimes a problem. Nonetheless, many service stations will do a pre-purchase check without an appointment because they are likely to lose the business otherwise. It's a good idea to get an inspection sheet stating any defects found or certifying that no defects were found.

A pre-purchase check usually costs \$50–\$100. A compression check is often extra and costs another \$50–\$100. An emissions check is also extra, and the price is sometimes set by the state. It will usually cost about the same as a pre-purchase check.

Certification

Certifying a used car is about the same as a pre-purchase inspection. A normal dealer certification also requires that everything is in working order. Thus, part of a certification is to make all necessary repairs, if any. Note, however, that a compression check is not necessarily part of a dealer certification.

Inspections on eBay

eBay over the years has attempted to arrange inexpensive pre-purchase inspections with various national companies. As a result, in 2003 it offered a pre-purchase inspection program through Pep Boys, a national vehicle maintenance and repair company with locations in 36 states. This inspection is $25 and provides you a nice computer read-out showing any problems with the vehicle. Again, the Pep Boys inspection does not include a cylinder compression check.

If the seller has done a Pep Boys check, or any other inspection by a reputable service station, ask him to send you a copy of the report. You will have to make a judgment as to whether such a report is acceptable for your purposes. If it isn't, insist on arranging your own inspection.

Colleague, Friend, or Relative

Have a colleague, friend, or family member check your vehicle for you in a distant city before you buy. In most cases, however, you won't have a friend or family member in such a distant city. So, if you're buying a collectible car, have a colleague in your collectors car club (the distant city chapter) go and look at the vehicle for you. Almost any club member will be happy to do so. The same goes for colleagues in boat clubs, RV clubs, and the like.

What Can Go Wrong?

Mr. Owens put together a list of the 3 major things that are the most likely to go wrong, when they are likely to go wrong, and what they cost to repair on the average.

1. Transmission failure; over 100,000 miles; $2,000 to $2,500.

2. Cylinder head gasket failure; as early as 60,000 miles but usually later; $700 to $1,700.

3. Air conditioning failure; as early as 30,000 miles but usually later; $700 to $800.

Mr. Owens put together a second is a list of the 9 minor things that are the most likely to go wrong, when they are likely to go wrong, and what they cost to repair on the average.

1. Water pump failure; 70,000 miles; $250 to $325.

2. Radiator failure; 70,000 miles; about $300.

3. Electrical failure; 80,000 miles; $200 to $325.

4. Oil leaks; as early as 50,000 miles but usually later; $100 to $300.

5. Heater core failure; as early as 50,000 miles but usually later; $300 to $400.

6. Fuel injector pump failure; as early as 40,000 miles but usually later; about $300.

7. Power steering fluid leaks; 70,000 miles; $150.

8. Computer failure; any time; $90 to $180.

9. Brake problems; as early as 30,000 miles but usually later; $175 to $275.

For Your Information

Mr. Owens stresses that these failures are all preventable by diligent routine maintenance; that is, lack of proper maintenance is usually the cause of these failures before 125,000 to 150,000 miles. The one exception is a vehicle computer. Note that some components for some vehices cost considerably above average to repair.

It's Worth Repeating

OK, we've said it before, but we'll say it again. If the seller will not allow your inspection of the vehicle and your mechanic's inspection of the vehicle as a contingency to the purchase *after the auction*, don't bid or otherwise make an offer to purchase the vehicle. Inspections are the best way to avoid undiscovered or undisclosed defects. Moreover, inspections are a prime means of avoiding fraud.

It's not unreasonable for a seller to require an earnest money payment due soon after the end of the auction. Try to inspect the vehicle before the payment is due if possible. If you can't make the inspections immediately and the earnest money payment is large, consider looking instead for another vehicle.

Paper Check

Physical inspections are fine, but a bureaucratic inspection (check) can be enlightening too. There are services that will check the records for you. Most states require paperwork to be submitted to provide a record of certain milestones in the life of a vehicle. These records are public, and certain services access these records to give you a report. All you need is the vehicle identification number (VIN) to get a report.

Accurate?

Are these reports accurate? Not necessarily. Sometimes the paperwork doesn't get done properly or is misplaced and does not enter the public record. The reports are more valuable for what they reveal than they are for establishing absolutely that a vehicle has a clean record. So, be careful. Don't rely completely on a record check.

The best practice is to call the DMV sometime prior to closing to make sure the vehicle doesn't have a salvage title.

CARFAX

For any purchase, whether local or on eBay, you can check the records to protect yourself. It's not expensive. Don't miss this opportunity to make your prospective transaction as safe as possible. Get a CARFAX Vehicle History Report (*http://www.carfax.com*), formerly known as the Lemon Check, to determine the history of the vehicle (see Figure 5.1).

Figure 5.1   The CARFAX website. ©2004 CARFAX inc.

CARFAX reports the following in its Vehicle History Report:

- Salvage history

- Odometer fraud

- Multiple owners

- Flood damage

- Major accident damage

- Fire damage

Review the report on any vehicle you are thinking about buying to make sure its history meets your satisfaction. If the seller provides the report, make sure the report has a recent date.

The Lemon Check Speaks

The first time Joe did a Lemon Check it was on an Isuzu Trooper that he was seriously considering buying. It showed a salvage title. This means that title to the vehicle had been taken by an insurance company that considered the vehicle totaled. The vehicle was then sold at a salvage auction to the seller (the person attempting to sell it to Joe). The seller repaired the vehicle and tried to sell it to Joe without disclosing the prior damage or the salvage title. The Trooper looked great and ran well. The questions are: How well was the vehicle repaired? Was there unrepaired structural damage that didn't show? Joe passed. He figured someone else can take the time to answer those questions. And he doesn't deal with people who are dishonest.

Note that a vehicle with a salvage title, assuming it runs well, is worth about half as much as the same vehicle with a normal title. You are unlikely to be able to finance a vehicle with a salvage title, and many insurance companies will not provide insurance for such vehicles. Yet there are a surprising number of vehicles with salvage titles for sale. Beware.

If the report shows that the ownership has changed hands several times, particularly if the vehicle is young, that might mean that something is wrong with the vehicle. It's a signal that you might want to investigate further.

Some southern states are notorious for their lax handling of the bureaucratic paperwork for vehicles. Certain owners take advantage of such situations to work mileage scams. If the title seems to have been transferred to a southern state (from outside the South) and then back to the original state with only small mileage changes, that may mean that the vehicle has much more mileage than shows on the odometer.

On eBay

eBay currently features AutoCheck to get history reports for vehicles. You can order them right from within eBay for $5 per report or $10 for 10 reports. They are similar to the CARFAX reports and should show the same public records (see Figure 5.2).

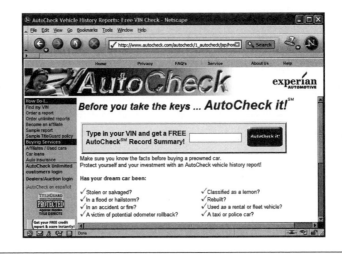

Figure 5.2   AutoCheck report. ©2003 Experian.

Never the Title

Never ask the seller for a copy of the vehicle title or for a copy of the CARFAX or AutoCheck report. This can possibly lead into a popular fraud scheme. Always run a report yourself instead. The seller can't forge a report you get directly from a reporting service.

More Paperwork

Also ask the seller to provide copies of maintenance receipts if available. You can get a picture of how well the seller cared for the vehicle. Many people do keep complete maintenance and repair records on their vehicles. However, this is like the CARFAX check. It is more reliable for the problems it shows, rather than to give the vehicle an absolute clean bill of health.

Published Information

There is no shortage of publications regarding vehicle quality and safety. Unfortunately, most published information is unreliable. It is indirectly financed by advertisers and consequently influenced by advertisers. In this section, we report on two sources of vehicle information we consider reliable and which do not rely on advertising dollars.

Consumer Reports

Consumer Reports is published by Consumers Union, a nonprofit organization. It has an unparalleled reputation for publishing reliable and unwhitewashed information about many products and specifically about vehicle quality and safety.

Other Consumer Publications

Don't confuse *Consumer Reports* with other publications that have "Consumer" in the title. Such other publications invariably do not go to the pain and expense to be totally objective as does *Consumer Reports*. In fact, some of them might be biased in favor of one advertiser (manufacturer) or another.

Each year *Consumer Reports* in its monthly magazine publishes a comprehensive report on used cars. It shows and evaluates their repair records to create a Reliability History. It makes it easy to separate the reliable cars from the lemons. In fact, the information that *Consumer Reports* publishes is quite extensive, and chances are you will be able to find information on the specific year and model of the car you are thinking of purchasing.

The Reliability History has 14 categories each of which are rated on a five-point scale:

1. Engine

2. Cooling

3. Fuel

4. Ignition

5. Transmission

6. Electrical

7. Air-conditioning

8. Suspension

9. Brakes

10. Exhaust

11. Paint/trim/rust

12. Body integrity

13. Power equipment

14. Body hardware

The Reliability History goes back eight years and is easy to read. It also includes a Reliability Verdict which is expressed as either high, average, or no rating.

In addition to the magazine report, *Consumer Reports* also publishes the *Used Car Buying Guide,* an annual book on the same topic, which you can buy in the bookstores. The book also includes Crash Test

Results on each vehicle and rates them on a five-point scale. This gives you an idea of how safe a car is.

Prices

The *Used Car Buying Guide* publishes vehicle prices too. Don't pay attention to such prices. They appear to be the high-end range of retail prices, and they will be outdated by the time you read them. In other words, they're way too high. *Consumer Reports* itself recommends that you use one of the pricing services or publications to determine value rather than use the prices it reports.

Most libraries have copies of both the magazines and the book. It's one of the most popular references in any library.

Use it. Or, take your chances. Joe's wife who always checks *Consumer Reports* fell in love with a 1999 Cadillac Catera available at a local dealership. A quick check in *Consumer Reports* indicated that the Catera is on *Consumer Reports* hit list of Reliability Risks, and Lani lost interest in the Catera quicker that you can say "lemon."

The Surprise Sale

Don got a call in September 2003 about a certain new model of Acura that was coming out in October. The prospective buyer wanted to buy one as soon as it was available. Don gave him a date in October when he expected it to be delivered. A few days before the date, Don heard by phone from the prospective buyer again. Don confirmed the date and the specific blue car that would be available.

The buyer insisted that he take delivery of the car immediately as soon as it was delivered to the dealership. Don said that it would take several hours to remove the stickers and detail the car. The prospective buyer said that wouldn't be necessary and that he would take the car as soon as it came off the truck. Don, the quintessential salesman who always aims to please said, "OK."

Then they got into a discussion about payment. The prospective buyer wanted to pay with a company check, but Don's dealership Acuras by Executive accepts only cashiers checks. The prospective buyer said that the dealership would undoubtedly accept his company check for the full sticker price and that he would fax a copy of it along with other documents the day before delivery. He told Don that if there was any problem with the check to call him immediately to get it resolved. Don agreed.

The day before delivery Don received by fax a number of documents including a copy of the company check. It came from *Consumer Reports*. The next day the *Consumer Reports* personnel arrived to claim the blue car and paid with a company check.

Consumer Reports resides in the general area where Don's dealership is located. Apparently they bought this new Acura model to test it for *Consumer Reports*. They like to take delivery before a dealer has an opportunity to make any alteration to it. They want it to be truly representative of all other identical model Acuras. And they want to pay full sticker price so that they cannot be accused of being bribed for a favorable report.

This story helps explain why *Consumer Reports* is such an esteemed source of information about vehicle quality and safety.

The *Used Car Buying Guide* is packed full of useful information on buying used cars. You will do well to use it in evaluating your used car purchase. It's available in most bookstores.

If you are a subscriber to *Consumer Reports*, you can access their website (*http://www.consumerreports.org*) and get much of the same information there.

J.D. Power and Associates

J.D. Power and Associates publishes a wealth of information and statistics for the automotive industry and for vendors to the automotive industry. Most of this information comes with a high price and is generally not available to consumers. Edmunds, however, on their website (*http://edmunds.com*) publishes the Power Circle Ratings for each car. These J.D. Power and Associates ratings come in three sets:

Initial Quality (0-90 days)
Mechanical Quality
Body & Interior Quality
Feature and Accessory Quality
Performance
Creature Comforts
Style

Midterm Reliability (1-3 years)
Mechanical Quality
Body & Interior Quality
Feature and Accessory Quality

Long Term Dependability (4-5 years)
Mechanical Quality
Body & Interior Quality
Feature and Accessory Quality

Each car is rated on a five-point scale. This is yet another source of unbiased information you can use to evaluate your prospective used car purchase. Go to the Edmunds website to check it out.

You can learn more about J.D. Power by going to its website (*http://www.jdpa.com*). Read more about Edmunds in Chapter 4.

Check Yourself

Most Americans love cars and trucks. It's so easy to get carried away when buying one. And impulse buying for cars and trucks, unlike for other merchandise, tends to linger for days instead of hours or minutes. Don't let impulse buying affect your rational approach to buying a vehicle on eBay. Don't take shortcuts. They usually lead to unnecessary risks. Do what you have to do to ensure that the vehicle you want to buy is in top shape. If you don't make a deal on one vehicle, you will find another good deal on eBay sooner or later.

Standard Procedure

Make an inspection; take a test drive, and a have a mechanic's inspection done as components of your standard procedure when purchasing a used vehicle. Make sure you review multiple photographs of the vehicle, run a vehicle history, and consult *Consumer Reports* before you travel to a distant city to buy it.

6

Financing

Financing is the fuel that makes the used car market run. The thing to remember is that when you use a loan to buy a vehicle, you're not just buying a vehicle. You're buying the financing too. You need to be just as careful buying the financing as you are buying the vehicle. This chapter will give you the background you need to choose financing that makes sense.

The 0 Interest Loan

In the fall of 2003 it seems there are a lot of 0 interest financing programs. Are they a benefit or a trick? Although this pertains essentially to new vehicle purchases, let's take a look anyway just for the instructional value.

New Vehicle

Suppose you want to buy a new SUV with a $35,000 sticker price. You calculate (based on your research) that you can buy it for $29,000 cash. You can borrow $29,000 from your bank at 8 percent interest payable over 5 years. Your payments will be $588 per month. The amount of interest you will pay over the 5-year period will be $6,280.

The dealership is offering a 0 percent loan on this vehicle. The only catch is that you have to pay the full price of $35,000 to qualify for the loan. The term is 5 years. That means that your payment will be $583 per month.

This is a wash. One deal is as good as the other. After two years you would owe $18,765 to your bank or $21,008 on the dealership financing. Thus, the bank loan balance would reduce a little faster, but otherwise the loans are about the same.

These examples illustrate three things. First, you need to calculate your choices accurately to compare them intelligently. Second, the difference in financing makes a difference in the deal. For instance, the difference between 0 percent and 8 percent financing is about a $6,000 of interest. Thus, you can see that financing is a major cost in purchasing a vehicle. Third, the financing is part of the total cost of purchasing a vehicle. In this case, the buyer could save $6,000 and get normal financing or spend $6,000 more and get special financing. Either way the buyer comes out about the same.

Change in Interest Rate

Let's change the numbers a little. Suppose the bank's interest rate in the above example is only 6 percent. Your payment will be $561 per month, and the amount of interest you pay over 5 years will be $4,639. This is an overall savings of about $1,400 over the dealership 0 interest loan deal. You can see that 2 percent makes a difference.

Loan Calculations

The 0 percent loans are usually reserved for new vehicles. But you can see in the last example that a 2 percent different in interest rate can mean a $1,400 difference in the cost of the vehicle. This is certainly relevant to purchasing a used vehicle. Consequently, we will provide you some tools in this chapter for making these kinds of calculations.

Calculating a Loan Payment

Use the loan payment table (see Table 6.1) to calculate your loan payment on loans of 1-7 years and interest rates of 0-14 percent. Multiply the payment multiplier times the loan amount. For instance, the multiplier for a 5-year loan at 6 percent is 0.019333. Multiply that times a loan amount of $29,000 (.019333 × 29000 = 560.651244), and you get a $560.65 per month payment. Round off to $561. Calculating a loan payment with the multipliers in the table is quite easy.

In the alternative, you can use the online loan calculator at the Automotive Mileposts website (see Figure 6.1):

http://automotivemileposts.com/ads/calculator.html

There is also a loan calculator on eBay Motors. If you know how to use one, you can also use a financial calculator to calculate loan payments, interest paid, and other loan calculations.

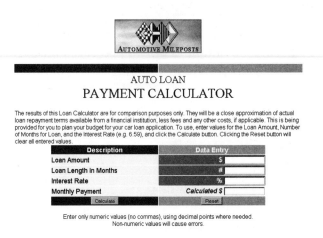

Figure 6.1   Online loan calculator. © 2000-2004 Automotive Mileposts Inc.

Table 6.1 Loan Amortization Payment Multipliers

	1 Year	2 Years	3 Years	4 Years	5 Years	6 Years	7 Years
0%	.083333	.041667	.027778	.020833	.016667	.013889	.011905
1%	.083785	.042102	.028208	.021261	.017094	.014316	.012331
2%	.084239	.042540	.028643	.021695	.017528	.014750	.012767
3%	.084694	.042981	.029081	.022134	.017969	.015194	.013213
4%	.085150	.043425	.029524	.022579	.018417	.015645	.013669
5%	.085607	.043871	.029971	.023029	.018871	.016105	.014134
6%	.086066	.044321	.030422	.023485	.019333	.016573	.014609
7%	.086527	.044773	.030877	.023946	.019801	.017049	.015093
8%	.086988	.045227	.031336	.024413	.020276	.017533	.015586
9%	.087451	.045685	.031800	.024885	.020758	.018026	.016089
10%	.087916	.046145	.032267	.025363	.021247	.018526	.016601
11%	.088382	.046608	.032739	.025846	.021742	.019034	.017122
12%	.088849	.047073	.033214	.026334	.022244	.019550	.017653
13%	.089317	.047542	.033694	.026827	.022753	.020074	.018192
14%	.089787	.048013	.034178	.027326	.023268	.020606	.018740

Calculating the Interest Paid

How do you figure out how much interest you pay over the full term of the loan? Add up all the payments made at the selected interest rate. Then subtract the loan amount.

In the example above, 60 payments of $561 adds up to $33,660 (60 × 561 = 33,660). Then subtract the loan amount of $29,000. The interest paid is $4,660 (33660 − 29000 = 4660).

Use the work sheet below to remind you how to make this calculation.

For ____ Percent Interest

Multiplier × Loan Amount = Monthly Payment

_____ × $_____ = $_____

Loan Term × Monthly Payment = Total Amount Paid

_____ × $_____ = $_____

Total Amount Paid – Loan Amount = Interest Paid

$_____ – $_____ = $_____

Go to the Exercise subsection later in the chapter to do an exercise, which calculates the interest paid. The answers to the exercise are as follows:

The 6 Percent Loan (4 years):

0.023485 × $11,000 = $258 payment amount per month.

48 × $258 per month = $12,384

$12,384 – $11,000 = $1,384 interest paid

The 7 Percent Loan (5 years):

0.019801 × $11,000 = $218 payment amount per month.

60 × $218 per month = $13,080

$13,080 – $11,000 = $2,080 interest paid

As you will find, your payments are $40 lower with the dealer loan but the total interest paid on the dealer loan is $708 higher.

Two Views

Buyers and sellers normally have two different views of vehicle financing. You want to make sure that your view, not the sellers, sets the terms of the financing.

The Dealer's View

For a dealer, financing is another way to make money. There are two ways a dealer can make money on a loan. First, the dealer can originate the loan. That is, a dealer can take the buyer through the process of applying for and obtaining a loan on the vehicle to be purchased. This is a convenience for both the dealer and the buyer. The dealer doesn't have to let the buyer out of sight (or out of control) before the sale is made. The buyer doesn't have to go anywhere else except the dealer showroom in order to buy the vehicle.

Second, the dealer can get a spread on the loan. That is, the dealer charges the buyer more interest than is necessary to obtain the loan and collects the difference. For example, suppose the dealer's financing source is willing to loan money to a particular buyer at six percent. The dealer charges the buyer eight percent and collects the two-percent difference (spread).

In fact, what often happens is that the dealer originates a vehicle loan and then sells the "paper" to a bank or financing company for a premium. The premium is calculated based on the origination work and the interest spread. Dealers can often make more profit providing financing than selling vehicles. That should tell you that it pays to shop for financing.

The Buyer's View

The key here is to understand that loan premium calculations are complex. You're unlikely to be able to do them yourself to determine what profit the dealer might be making so as to help you negotiate. So, how can you get the best deal? As a practical matter, the only thing you can do is shop. That means shop around for the best deal on a loan.

Unfortunately, many buyers make a loan decision on just one loan criteria, the monthly payment. This is the worst possible way to make a financial decision. Certainly the monthly payment is important, but there are many roads to get there. Suppose you decide that the highest monthly payment you can make on a vehicle is $260. See Table 6.2 below, which shows what that might mean in regard to purchasing dollars.

Table 6.2 Various Loans at a Constant Monthy Payment

Monthly Payment	Interest	Term (months)	Loan Amount	Interest Paid
$260	6%	36	$8,546	$813
$260	6%	48	$11,070	$1,409
$260	6%	60	$13,448	$2,151
$260	6%	72	$15,688	$3,031
$260	7%	36	$8,420	$939
$260	7%	48	$10,857	$1,622
$260	7%	60	$13,130	$2,469
$260	7%	72	$15,250	$3,469

Current interest rates are around six or seven percent for a person with your credit rating. The car you are buying has a $12,500 retail value (based on your research), and your goal is to buy it for $11,000. The dealer is asking $13,900. You will finance 100 percent of the purchase price.

The dealer makes you an offer. She says, "You can drive it away right now for $260 per month on a five-year loan at 6 percent interest. And that's about as good an interest rate as you're going to find in this town." How much are you paying for the car? If you look at the chart, you'll see you're paying $13,448 for it, somewhat more than you wanted to pay and more than it's worth.

So, what's your next counteroffer? A good one might be, "That sounds good. Let's make that a four-year term and you've got a deal." That would make the price of the car $11,070, just about what you want to pay.

Notice on the chart that a change in interest rate doesn't make a huge difference. But a change in length of the loan changes the purchase price considerably. Dealers love to sell vehicles based on how much a customer can pay each month. And they'll make a loan right in the office while you're talking to them.

Instant Loans

Even in bygone years, a dealer could make a vehicle loan pretty quickly. Today they can make one almost instantly. Once you've agreed to something, you won't have a lot of time to mull it over. Maybe five minutes. You had better consider it carefully and unhurriedly before you agree.

Buyer's Strategy

A good strategy for buyers is simply to consider any financing separately from the purchase of the vehicle. In fact, the best way to negotiate is to let the seller know that you will pay cash for the vehicle. How do you do that? You line up financing ahead of time.

If you're a member of a credit union, you will probably get favorable financing there. Banks are competitive too. Finance companies usually loan to higher risk buyers and usually charge higher interest rates in general. Dealers loan money too, but they sell their paper to a bank. Thus, the bank is the real lender. You can expect dealer's rates to be anywhere from identical to bank rates to much higher than bank rates.

Dealers brag that they can beat credit union rates, and in many cases they can. Whether or not they can depends on the bank behind them. In any event, you will likely get a good loan from a dealer only if you negotiate it well, but make sure you negotiate it separately from the purchase of the vehicle. Note that usually a credit union does automatic payment deductions from your account at the first of the month. A bank doesn't normally do so, and you can usually pay as late as the 15th of the month without penalty.

What About Other Dealer Financing?

The automobile manufacturers have finance companies such as GMAC (General Motors Acceptance Corporation). Such finance companies also buy dealer paper just like banks do. That gives certain dealers a financing option in addition to banks.

Manufacturers also offer special financing with reduced interest rates or even a 0 percent interest rate. Such special financing is usually only available for the purchase of new vehicles, however, and you may not be able to get such financing for a used vehicle. Were you to get such financing for a used vehicle, you would undoubtedly have to pay the dealer's asking price for the vehicle. And we know that means a substantially higher purchase price.

Arrange Ahead

If you walk in to buy a vehicle with your financing already lined up and can, in effect, pay cash for a vehicle, you are in a strong negotiating position. Negotiate the purchase of a vehicle as if you are going to pay cash.

Once you have reached agreement on the purchase price, there's no reason you can't take a look at what the dealer will offer you in the way of loan terms. If it beats what you have lined up already, finance the vehicle through the dealer. But whatever you do, don't evaluate the loan based solely on how much the payment is.

What's the problem with making the terms of the loan the focus of negotiation? It's simply this. The dealer has the knowledge and expertise to negotiate financial arrangements. And you don't. It's not your expertise. Why get involved in a negotiation in which the other party has a substantial advantage?

Exercise

Here's a situation where you can use the interest expense calculation you learned earlier in this chapter. *The correct answer is earlier in the chapter at the end of the Calculating the Interest Paid subsection.*

You negotiate to purchase a used minivan with 24,000 miles for $11,000 ($500 above the wholesale value). You plan to finance the full purchase price. Your credit union offers you a loan at 6 percent interest for 48 months. After you have negotiated the purchase price with the dealer, the dealer offers you a loan at 7 percent for 60 months. What are the payments for each loan? How much interest do you pay on each loan, assuming you make payments for the full term of each loan? Use the work sheet provided in the Calculating the Interest Paid subsection.

Now which of these loans will you take? Higher payments for four years but less total interest paid. Or, Lower payments for five years but more total interest paid. There is no right answer to this question. But until you've done the calculations, you don't have enough information to make an intelligent decision.

What's to Be Financed?

What does it mean to finance the purchase price? Does it include sales tax? Does it include license fees? Does it include the new sound system you're having installed in the vehicle? And who decides what it will include?

To understand how to answer this question, you must understand how a banker thinks.

The Buyer's Credit Rating

The buyer's credit rating determines the amount of the loan and the interest rate at which the loan will be made. The worse the credit rating, the more risk in the loan. The more risk in the loan, the less the loan amount and the higher the interest rate.

Lenders each create their own scoring system based on buyer credit characteristics. The score a particular buyer gets determines the amount of the loan and the interest rate for a specific purchase.

A Vehicle as Collateral

A vehicle makes pretty good collateral. Generally it can be repossessed easily in the event of default and resold for a reasonable price. As a result, it is not difficult to get 100 percent financing, assuming you have good credit.

Oddly enough, vehicle financing is widely available, even for those with bad credit. That's only because vehicles are good collateral. If you went bankrupt yesterday, you can get a vehicle loan today. The interest rate will be much higher than normal. But even so, you can get the loan.

Blue Book

The lender looks at the blue book value. Each lender is different, and each lender may use a different brand of blue book. Remember the discussion of blue book values in Chapter 4. Our experience is that a lender will loan an amount equal to a price halfway between the wholesale and retail values (what Edmunds calls the Private Party sales price).

Of course, if your net worth is $2,000,000, you have no debt, and your discretionary income is $5,000 a month, the bank might use the event of a $20,000 vehicle purchase to loan you $30,000. After all, the bank is in business to make money, and you're a pretty good credit risk even without the vehicle as collateral. But most of us don't fall into such a creditworthy category. So, what is a realistic amount to borrow?

Most of us with good credit can borrow up to the Private Party sales price. Consequently, if you pay more than that price, you will have to make a down payment to cover the difference. If you pay less than that price, it opens the opportunity to cover other transactional expenses with the loan besides just the purchase price.

Let's go back to our van example. You purchase a used minivan with 24,000 miles for $11,000 ($500 above the wholesale value). The retail value is $13,500 and the Private Party value is $12,000. You need an $11,000 loan to purchase the van. The lender is willing to loan you $12,000. This gives you the opportunity to include the sales tax in the loan. At 8 percent, the sales tax will be $880, and you can borrow a little bit more than enough to cover it.

The good news is when you buy a car at about $2,500 under wholesale, as Joe did for his wife recently, you can finance the purchase price, the sales tax, a warranty, and the license fee. The bad news is that you have to make higher payments.

Know the Expenses

What are the major expenses you can cover with a loan above the purchase price?

- Sales tax

- License fee

- Warranty

- New equipment installation (e.g., sunroof)

- New tires

- Needed repairs

I'm sure in the history of horse (auto) trading more imaginative things have been included, but the above list gives you some of the common expenses that are routinely covered. It also gives you an idea of some of the things you will have to pay for out of pocket if the loan does not cover them.

This raises an important point. You have to know all the expenses associated with buying a vehicle or else you may be surprised. Specifically, you have to be ready to pay all the expenses not covered by the loan. Otherwise, you may have to default on an agreement and perhaps forfeit an earnest money deposit. The purchase price is just one the components of a purchase, and there are other components, each with a price tag.

Less Than Perfect Credit

You may have less than perfect credit through no fault of your own. When you have no credit history or have recently had a lengthy period of unemployment, or for some other reason beyond your control, you may not be able to get the loan you need at a reasonable interest rate. That may not mean you can't get any loan at a decent interest rate. It may just mean that you have to put some money down to purchase your next vehicle. In fact, the more money you put down, the more likely you are to get an attractive loan, albeit a smaller loan than you want.

As mentioned before, the best time to find out how much you can borrow at a reasonable interest rate is before you go shopping for a vehicle. At best you want to be able to negotiate as a cash buyer. At worst you want to avoid being at the mercy of the dealership financial department or a finance company, neither of which are known to be merciful.

And eBay?

Hey, this is a book about eBay Motors. And at the end of the chapter we're finally getting around to mentioning it. Why's that? Well, financing is no different on the eBay world than in the offline world.

Prepare

The primary task at hand is to line up your financing before you bid. You can't take a chance bidding on a vehicle without knowing specifically how you will pay for the vehicle. If you win the auction and can't get financing—or can't get enough financing—then you might have to abort the transaction subjecting yourself to negative feedback.

Another reason to line up your financing ahead of your bidding is that although many vehicle auctions are listed by dealers that might be able to assist you in getting financing, most eBay sellers are private parties who can give you little assistance. While it is true that several financing sources advertise on eBay Motors, they are just additional funding sources to your local financial institutions. They offer nothing special. So, your first job as a vehicle buyer is to line up financing before you bid.

Homework

Many of us procrastinate even as we start to plow through the listings looking for our next vehicle. Then, we spot something that's fits our requirements. Now the game is on. But unfortunately, we're not prepared. The auction is over in 24 hours, and we don't know yet if the credit union will loan us any money, or if so at what interest rate.

To be successful on eBay Motors, you have to do your homework. That means finding financing ahead of bidding.

Summary

Financing is a dealer's game. Don't play the game on the dealer's home field. Insist on negotiating the financing your way.

At least shop around for the best financing available, negotiate the financing separate from the purchase, and don't base your decision solely on the amount of the monthly payment. It doesn't hurt to analyze the financing, too, with the processes provided in this chapter.

Make sure you've lined up financing before you bid even if you might eventually use another finaicing source. And be ready to pay the costs of a purchase transaction that may not be covered by financing.

7

Insurance

Insurance is not exactly the most exciting topic, but your life may take on some unwanted agony someday if you don't pay attention to motor vehicle insurance.

The first rule of car insurance in regard to an eBay vehicle purchase is to make sure you have it before the transaction closes. Duh! But think about it. There are a lot of details to take care of when you buy a vehicle. And when you buy it in a distant city to which you will travel to take delivery, you have all the travel details to worry about too. Of course you don't want to take on the obligation to pay for insurance until you're sure you own the purchased vehicle. So, it's one of the last details on your list. But it's a detail you don't want to overlook.

The second rule of vehicle insurance is to take the opportunity of purchasing a vehicle to review your coverage. When was the last time you reviewed your insurance coverage? What has happened in your life since then that might warrant additional coverage, or perhaps even a decrease in coverage? You can do this any time, of course, but the purchase of a vehicle is a good time to think about it and make any appropriate changes.

Types of Insurance

Below are the normal types of insurance that together as a package make up what we know as auto insurance. You don't have to buy coverage for all types of insurance, but many people do buy complete coverage.

Collision Insurance

This simply covers the damage to your vehicle in an accident. This is expensive because we seem to damage vehicles occasionally over the years. At some point, the damage to a vehicle is so extensive that it costs more to fix it than to buy a replacement vehicle (of the same year, same model). We then say the vehicle is "totaled." The insurance company then pays the replacement value, normally the retail price as published by the pricing services (see Chapter 4). There is usually no specific dollar limit on this coverage, but the value of your vehicle is taken into consideration in setting the amount of the premium.

Comprehensive

This is a grab bag of coverages such as for theft, fire, hail, flood, glass damage, vandalism, and the like.

Medical

This coverage pays the medical bills of you and the people injured in your vehicle. There is typically a dollar limit, such as $5,000.

Liability (Bodily Injury)

The liability we need to protect against is liability for personal injury resulting from an accident. To repair or replace vehicles is cheap compared to repairing human beings. And liability insurance covers those sad accidents where someone is severely injured. Fault is assigned to one of the parties in an accident. If that party is you, you will be liable for the personal injuries suffered by the other party (driver), the passengers in the other vehicle, and perhaps even the passengers in your own vehicle.

Note that this does not cover you—you can't sue yourself. Additionally, it doesn't cover members of your own family riding in your vehicle, unless they sue you.

There is a dollar limit on liability coverage expressed as dollars per injured person and dollars per accident. Thus, 250/500 coverage means that the insurance company will pay up to $250,000 per injured person with a limit of $500,000 per accident.

Your state may have a requirement that you carry minimum coverage. Such requirements range from 10/20 to 50/100.

Property Damage

This is for damage you do to someone else's property, such as a vehicle or building. The coverage has a dollar limit and is often included with liability. For instance, 250/500/100 means $250,000 per person, $500,000 per accident, and $100,000 for property damage.

Uninsured Motorist

If the other party is at fault but has no insurance or has inadequate insurance, your uninsured motorist coverage will pay as if the other party had your insurance coverage. In other words, your coverage becomes theirs, and your insurance company will pay you as if it were the insurance company for the other party.

Umbrella

This coverage insures you against claims above and beyond your maximum liability coverages provided by your basic insurance. The coverage goes up to a certain designated amount. Thus, if you get a $1,000,000 umbrella policy (umbrella coverage usually is usually in increments of a million dollars), it takes your other liability coverages up to $1,000,000. This isn't terribly expensive, and it's a good idea to get it if you can afford it. Note, however, that it is not included in uninsured motorist coverage.

No-Fault

About half of the states have no-fault vehicle insurance. This is a different insurance system than the traditional vehicle insurance system. Therefore, you need special insurance. If you live in a no-fault state, consult with your insurance agent in order to understand your coverage.

Amount of Coverage

What amount of coverage do you need? What deductible is adequate? These are two important financial questions.

Coverage

The question of the amount of coverage has to do with liability insurance. You want to protect your assets. If you have $20,000 in assets, you don't need much insurance. If someone sues you and gets a judgment in excess of your insurance coverage, you only have $20,000 to lose. You can declare bankruptcy and start over.

However, if you have $200,000 in assets (e.g., the equity in your home), you don't want to get a judgment in excess of your coverage because you have $200,000 to lose. It might be tough to build your assets back up to $200,000 after declaring bankruptcy. The only way to avoid such a situation is to have enough coverage to make it unlikely that any judgment from a personal injury law suit will exceed your coverage. Let's look at some examples.

> Suppose you have 250/500 coverage. You cause an accident and one victim gets a $420,000 personal injury judgment against you. What does the insurance cover? It covers only $250,000 of the $420,000 judgment.

> Suppose you have the same coverage as above. You cause an accident, and two victims each get a $375,000 judgment against you. What does the insurance cover? It covers only $500,000 of the total judgments ($750,000).

> Suppose you have the same coverage as above. You hit a bus and eight victims get a total of $1,236,000 of judgments against. What does the insurance cover? It covers only $500,000.

You might note that the accident scenarios presented are not unusual examples. We've all heard of accident victims getting judgments for outrageous amounts. Also note that $2,000,000 of umbrella coverage would have insulated you against any person financial loss.

Another View

Another way to look at auto insurance coverage is from a moral point of view. The primary mechanism our society uses to take care of victims of accidents is the tort-insurance system; that is, the legal blame together with insurance coverage takes care of people's injuries. In order to provide adequate compensation to victims of accidents you might cause, you should carry hefty insurance coverage. Should your insurance (plus your assets) not cover a victims' reasonable compensation for injuries, he or she may have nowhere else to turn to pay for medical and disability expenses. Don't under insure. It's not good for victims as well as being potentially unhealthy for your personal estate.

What's Missing?

What's missing is coverage for you! If you are at fault, you get no compensation for serious injuries except for medical coverage.

If the other party is at fault but is not insured adequately, you may not get enough compensation for serious injuries. Suppose you have uninsured motorist coverage and 250/500 for liability. You sustain damages (medical and disability costs) of $800,000. Your insurance company will pay only up to $250,000. Even if you have an umbrella policy, it will pay only up to that limit.

Family Members

Presumably, family members are in the same position that you are. However, family members can theoretically sue you, which would put them in the same position of non-family members.

What can you do to remedy this situation? You need to have good health insurance and adequate disability insurance. But even that coverage may be inadequate to sustain you through serious injuries.

Deductible

What deductible you choose depends on how much cash you usually have on hand and how much risk you want to take. For instance, with $50 deductible, you will be fully covered for all claims except for the first $50. Fifty dollars isn't much today, so $50 deductible is essentially full coverage.

On the other hand, $500 deductible will cover all but the first $500 of a claim. However, $500 is a substantial sum that will put a big dent in many budgets. If you can't cover such a deductible out of your normal monthly budget or savings, you may have no choice except to pay extra for a lower deductible that will protect you against large losses.

The first dollars of any coverage are the most expensive to insure. When you raise the deductible, you are self-insuring more of the first dollars, the most expensive insurance. Consequently, you can reduce your insurance premiums substantially by raising your deductible.

As you raise your deductible, you get closer to the point where you may no longer be said to have normal insurance. You have only *catastrophic* insurance. For instance, if you elect to have $5,000 deductible on your auto insurance, it will take a substantial claim (an almost catastrophic claim) to generate any insurance payoff.

We recommend a catastrophic deductible if you're a good driver and can afford to cover a large deductible should a claim materialize. Otherwise you're better off to pay more for a low deductible.

Review

As mentioned at the beginning of the chapter, the occasion of buying a vehicle is a good time to sit down and review your coverage. Your assets may have increased considerably since the last time you thought about insurance coverage, and now might be the time to get an umbrella policy. There also many other factors that may have changed and will affect the amount of coverage you need.

Shop

The occasion of buying a vehicle is a good time to shop for new insurance if you think you might be able to get a better deal. Joe has had auto insurance with the same company for 17 years. Nonetheless, he normally shops a little just to make sure he continues to get good insurance rates and coverage. And usually shopping for insurance comes to mind at the time he buys his next car.

Timing

As an owner, you are responsible for your vehicle. That responsibility starts the minute you become the owner of the vehicle.

Existing Policy

Many vehicle insurance policies have provisions that automatically insure you for a period (e.g., 30 days) after you buy a vehicle. Check your policy (call your insurance agent) to see if yours does. If so, don't rely on such a provision without notifying your insurance agent.

You need to call your insurance agent as soon as the transaction closes and inform her that you have another vehicle. Provide the VIN and the normal information on about the vehicle. Double check to make sure you have coverage.

What we usually do is have our agent switch insurance from the vehicle we're going to sell to the vehicle we're buying. That way, the insurance agent has specific information on the new vehicle, and it's clear that coverage exists. Then, we still have 30 days grace coverage on the vehicle we're going to sell. (If we can't sell within the 30 days, we have to pay for another policy.) Every insurance company is different, so make sure you contact your insurance agent before completing the purchase transaction.

No Existing Policy

If you don't have insurance coverage, you need to line it up ahead of time. It must be in effect as soon as you take ownership of the vehicle, even if the vehicle is to be shipped to you. This can be tricky. If you don't close on the vehicle because of one thing or another, you don't want to pay for unnecessary insurance, even for a week. If you do close, you want to have coverage immediately after the closing. We will leave it to you to work things out with your insurance agent. Conveniently there are several auto insurance companies on eBay Motors. You might check them out when you look for coverage.

Mandatory

Having coverage as soon as you become the owner is mandatory. Indeed, in most states it's illegal to drive a vehicle without minimum liability insurance. But it's also mandatory from a risk point of view. It's not smart to take a chance driving without insurance. Make sure you have the coverage you need before you become the owner.

Summary

Don't overlook obtaining proper insurance coverage for your purchase. It's easy to forget something as mundane as insurance in the heat of closing a vehicle transaction, particularly when you're in a distant city worrying about other closing details. Make sure you set up to get coverage well in advance of the closing, and make sure that the coverage goes into effect just as soon as you become the new owner.

8

Bidding

The tips for effective bidding are the same as for any bidding on eBay. Bidding on vehicles doesn't require special techniques. Bidding on a vehicle, however, can be a very emotional endeavor. Why? It takes preparation and commitment. It's a big ticket item. Once you've made your choice to bid, there's a lot riding on the outcome.

Research

As we and most other experts have said, knowing the value is the most effective bidding technique. That takes research. But first you have to decide what you want.

Choice

As suggested in Chapter 2, you have to decide which vehicle is for you. That brings focus and realism to your buying efforts, and you really have to decide before you can bid rationally.

Price

Once you've decided what you want, you need to research the value of the vehicle. You need to get a good idea of what purchase price you are likely to pay. Without making a choice and ascertaining value, your bidding effort will be aimless, ineffective, or subject to irrational impulse.

Preparation

There are a lot of things you might do to prepare to bid, such as arrange auto insurance, but there's one thing you must do. That's arrange financing. You can't bid confidently without knowing how you will pay for the vehicle. And if you win the bidding and can't pay for the vehicle, you'll get negative feedback. Consequently, you have to be sure that you have the means to pay the purchase price prior to bidding.

Some people have a good credit rating and have been doing business with the same financial institution for so long that they know they will have financing to buy any vehicle, at any time they choose. This is not an uncommon situation. Nonetheless, many other people have to get tentative approval—or even explicit approval—from their financial institution to ensure that they will have the money to complete the purchase transaction. You need to assess your situation and make sure that the money will be available when you need it to complete your vehicle purchase.

Bidding Techniques

The bidding techniques for vehicle auctions are no different than any other auctions except for the requisite preparation outlined above. See *eBay the Smart Way* for a comprehensive discussion of bidding.

It is sufficient to say here that knowing the value is the best bidding technique. Nothing beats this technique for effectiveness.

By researching via the pricing services and by checking the eBay archives, you will have a pretty good idea of a vehicle's worth. Then you have to decide what it's worth to you. These could be two different values, although if you're realistic and really desire to buy a vehicle, the market value and your value are usually the same.

Once you know the top purchase price you will pay, bidding becomes reasonably simple. Nonetheless, you have to understand that the highest bidder wins the auction. If someone else is willing to bid more than you, they are almost certain to win the auction no matter what bidding techniques you use. In other words, to get outbid by someone willing to bid higher than you is not a condemnation of your bidding skills. It is simply a fact of life like the law of gravity.

Proxy Bidding

Without proxy bidding, you will have to show up for the end of the auction and get into a bidding showdown if there are other bidders.

With proxy bidding (built into the eBay system), eBay will do your bidding for you up to to your maximum bid. But see New Rule subsection below.

Armed with these ideas, you can bid confidently once you've determined your maximum purchase price. If you lose, you lose. It's not your fault.

Emotional Impact

Where bidding on vehicles differs from other eBay items is in the inherent emotion that accompanies bidding on eBay Motors. What causes the emotion? Well, first of all, buying a vehicle is a major event for most people. Vehicles cost a lot of money and require a substantial financial commitment.

Second Largest

For many people, a vehicle is the second largest purchase they will make in a lifetime, ranking after their house.

Second, there is a strong emotional element in one's choice of vehicles. If one's choice goes unfulfilled, it's a letdown. Third, it takes work to prepare to bid. At the least, you have to line up financing, research values, and go through the emotional gyrations to make an emotionally sound choice. By the time you're ready to bid, you have already made a big commitment. Perhaps the only thing that saves the day should you lose the bidding on a vehicle is the fact that there are or will soon be more identical vehicles available on eBay.

Bidding on big-ticket items is a serious business. Be prepared to deal with the emotional impact that such bidding might bring.

New Rule

Be advised—perhaps we should say beware—that there is a new bidding rule that pertains only to eBay Motors. *Proxy bidding is suspended.* What you bid is what you will see as the high bid (assuming you are the high bidder). Once the reserve has been reached, the proxy bidding resumes. In other words, the proxy bidding is suspended only for bidding up to the reserve but not over.

A Controversy

The authors cannot agree on one aspect of eBay Motors auctions. That seems natural. Joe is essentially a buyer, and Don is essentially a seller. So, what's this all about?

Buyer's Position

It's the buyer's position that a potential buyer puts in significant preparation before bidding on a vehicle (e.g., arranges financing). If the seller stops the auction after the potential buyer has bid or even before the potential buyer bids, it's not fair to the potential buyer. Indeed, it's very irritating to the potential buyer.

In addition, everyone knows the reason the seller stops the auction. The seller has found a serious buyer, but not necessarily the highest bidder. The potential buyers who are bidding and playing by the spirit of the eBay rules may be willing to pay more for the vehicle than the buyer with whom the seller is negotiating a purchase. But the potential buyers are preempted from buying the vehicle.

Seller's Position

The seller's position is that it's perfectly legal according to eBay rules to stop an auction. If a serious buyer materializes as a result of the auction, or due to offline advertising, the seller should be able to start and conclude negotiations immediately with such a buyer before the auction is over.

It's primarily dealers who take this position. Sometimes this is stated in their auction ad and sometimes not. In any event, it is a wide spread practice. At first look, it seems like a self-defeating practice. Why not wait to see what the high bid will be? But "a bird in the hand is worth two in the bush" seems to be the ultimate guiding principle.

eBay's Position

We can't speak for eBay, but it appears that eBay is set up to support the seller's position whether willingly or unwillingly. The normal fee structure does not apply to eBay Motors. (The eBay Motors fixed insertion fee and fixed transaction service fee look more like an advertising fee; there is no final value fee.) It is an advertising fee, in effect, for dealers.

To eBay's credit, it has done away with the proxy bidding (up to the reserve) in order to show higher bids earlier in the auction, presumably to keep the seller from stopping the auction prematurely. eBay has also made a tremendous effort to provide extensive benefits to buyers and has been surprisingly successful in doing so. Such benefits are not available to transactions outside eBay, so they will work to keep the transactions on eBay.

Solution

What's the solution for buyers? Until the system changes, the first step is to identify the seller. If the seller is a private party, then bid and continue bidding as you would in any auction. Private parties are not as likely as dealers to stop their auctions.

If the seller is a dealer, apparently the name of the game is to contact the dealer immediately and negotiate an off-eBay deal. Call the dealer and insist on an immediate negotiation. If the negotiation is successful, insist that the seller stop the auction. If you don't follow this course of action, another buyer probably will.

In reality, not all the vehicles auctioned on eBay actually sell. Thus, the dealer-stopped-auction practice should not be a problem for the eBay Motors auctions where there are no buyers.

Conclusion

There is an anomaly in the eBay system caused by the realities of the used car business. It is important that a dealer strike a deal with the first person who makes a serious offer to buy the vehicle. There may not be a second person who will make a serious offer. This is reinforced by the fact that not all vehicles offered on eBay Motors sell. Hence, it is likely that the practice by dealers of stopping auctions will continue unless eBay institutes a penalty for it.

Other Items

Cancelling auctions is not confined to eBay Motors. It also takes place in auctions for other eBay items, particularly big ticket items. More often than not, it seems it's a retailer, not a private party, who cancels an auction.

A Buying Experience

Joe needs a 4-wheel-drive (4WD) vehicle to drive the dirt roads and jeep trails to reach the trailheads where he starts his treks into the wilderness. His 1987 Isuzu Trooper 4WD had 198,000 miles on it in the summer of 2000 and was still running well, but he knew that if anything major went wrong with the vehicle, it would not be worth repairing.

It didn't seem prudent to him to buy a new Trooper because the thought of leaving a new $35,000 vehicle at a trailhead 90 miles from the nearest pavement for ten days at a time seemed a little too risky for him. Therefore, he wanted to buy a 1992–1997 Trooper in top condition with low mileage for which he expected to pay $7,000-$14,000.

The San Francisco Bay Area where he lives has about seven million people. Even in this huge market, he had few good choices in Troopers. But on eBay he often found Troopers he would buy (before he was ready to buy), and the winning bids were often at or below wholesale price. An unusual number of these acceptable Troopers auctioned on eBay were in Texas 2,000 miles away. He figured he could pick up a vehicle in Texas himself for $600 in travel expenses or have it shipped for about the same cost. With a purchase at or below wholesale, the cost of delivery made sense, and he would get exactly what he wanted. Therefore, eBay offered a solid marketplace in which to seriously seek a vehicle.

Why so fussy? Why not some other 4WD vehicle? Joe is very partial to Troopers and was not willing to settle for anything else. Had he been willing to purchase any comparable 4WD, it would have been much easier to find a vehicle at home.

Local Action

Starting in August, he regularly checked a local car mart (weekend auto sales in a municipal parking lot), local auto sales publications, metro classifieds, and Web classified listings. In addition, he had a local used car dealer looking for a Trooper at the regional auto auctions for him.

He had checked Trooper auctions on eBay every couple of weeks starting in March just to observe. He saw many Troopers he might have purchased, but he wasn't ready to buy yet. In preparation for a potential immediate purchase, he started checking Trooper auctions on eBay three times a week in early August. Which would it be, an eBay purchase or a local purchase?

He continued watching Trooper auctions on eBay through the second week of October and continued to look for a Trooper locally. He found AutoTrader and Cars.com to be very useful in finding online vehicle classifieds for his locale. He found the metro newspapers and other print publications almost useless.

From the beginning of August until the first week of October, there was only one Trooper (near Chicago) on eBay on which he bid. He was outbid by a little bit in the preliminary bidding the day before the auction ended. He might have been competitive in the last few minutes of the auction. Unfortunately he had an important four-hour meeting that prevented him from participating. (We don't recommend absentee bidding on expensive items such as vehicles.)

During this entire period, there was a paucity of Troopers on eBay. For one whole day there was not even one. For one week there were only two. It was very discouraging.

Joe got so desperate that he even drove to Napa, not far away, to see a six-year-old Trooper listed in AutoTrader (without a price) by a dealer. It turned out to be in good condition but with high mileage and a price that was *twice* the blue book retail! He didn't even bother to make inquiries.

Through AutoTrader he found a Trooper in San Francisco. He drove into the city to see it early on a Saturday evening and got caught in a traffic jam, which added two hours to his one-way trip. Consequently, it was dark when he inspected the Trooper. Four days later he tried to make an offer on it. In the phone conversation it came out that the Trooper had no backseat. In the dark he had assumed that the backseat was folded down; instead, it wasn't there at all. Scratch another possibility.

Suddenly a 1994 Trooper in Dallas appeared on eBay (minimum bid about $1,500 under blue book wholesale with no reserve). It was a little fancier than he wanted and it had normal mileage for its age. It was offered by a used car dealer. About the same time he also found a local Trooper on AutoTrader at a good price with low mileage. He wanted to see the local Trooper before bidding on the Dallas Trooper. By the time he had inspected and test driven the local Trooper, the dealer had pulled the Dallas Trooper off eBay. No one had yet bid on it. There were only nine hours left until the end of the auction when Joe logged onto eBay Motors to make his bid, but the Dallas Trooper was gone.

Notify the Dealer

As a practical matter, if you want to buy a vehicle be sure to let the seller know well before the auction is over. You can follow the dealer's lead on how to handle the purchase. The dealer may want to wait until the end of the auction or may want to sell immediately off eBay. Or, you can insist on starting negotiations off eBay immediately.

So, he missed making his bid on the Dallas Trooper and ended up making a deal on the local Trooper (found through AutoTrader) instead. He and the seller had an appointment to take the vehicle in for a pre-purchase inspection by a mechanic in the seller's neighborhood (at Joe's expense), a condition of the purchase deal. The day before the inspection, the seller, who had not asked for a deposit or writtem contract, called to say that he had sold the vehicle to someone else who had put down a $500 deposit on the vehicle. Scratch another deal. Ironically, this Trooper had been on AutoTrader for five weeks without anyone showing any interest.

As for the local used car dealer who attempted to find Joe a Trooper at the regional auto auctions, he finally found one and bought it for Joe at a good price. Unfortunately, although Joe almost never sees a Trooper he doesn't like, he didn't like this one. It had an odor, which was unidentifiable. The odor seemed quite unpleasant to him, although no one else would admit to being able to smell it. The odor did it. This Trooper was not meant for Joe. Fortunately, the dealer never buys a vehicle he can't sell off his lot at a profit. Consequently, he was amenable to letting Joe off the hook in regard to their informal purchase agreement, and Joe didn't buy it.

Smelling Is Believing

The Trooper Joe rejected was a very nice vehicle. But it illustrates an important point. Even though vehicles are much the same, they are different too. In this case, Joe couldn't live with the odor. If you obligate yourself to a purchase before an inspection, you want to have an out.

Soon thereafter Joe found a 1995 Trooper in AutoTrader that he purchased from a private party for $12,300. It was a fancier model than he wanted but was in top condition with 55,000 miles, and he bought it for $800 over blue book wholesale; this was somewhat below the midpoint between wholesale and retail. Thus ended his ten-week search.

Later when he put his old Trooper up for auction on eBay Motors, he found several nice Troopers that he might have purchased that seemed to be priced lower than the one he bought. This proves that had he been more patient, he may have made a better purchase. The ten-week period that he searched for Troopers on eBay turned out to be something of an unusual Trooper drought.

Read about a successful eBay Motors vehicle buying experience in Chapter 17.

What does this automotive saga illustrate? First, although eBay is a huge market, it is still just one of several alternative markets where you might find the vehicle you want. Not every attempt to buy a vehicle on eBay will be successful. Second, eBay's marketplace size in regard to a specific brand and model (e.g., 1995 Trooper) expands and contracts each week. With a little patience, you are more likely to find the vehicle you want than if you have to buy immediately.

Note that eBay Motors has four times as many vehicles listed today as when Joe was looking for a Trooper.

Summary

Bidding for a vehicle is much the same as bidding for any eBay item except that:

- You need to be prepared before you bid.

- The proxy bidding is a little different.

- Dealers are making deals off eBay and cancelling auctions.

As a buyer strategy, you may want contact the seller as soon as you decide to bid on a vehicle, even before you're ready to bid. You can play it from there according to the situation.

9

Warranties

A warranty is just an insurance policy that pays off if the vehicle breaks down. A warranty varies in what it covers, for how long, and for how many miles. Most vehicles come with a manufacturer's warranty. Such warranties vary greatly, but typically a manufacturer's warranty covers some types of breakdowns for the first four years or 48,000 miles. If you buy a used vehicle, you will want to make sure that you get the remaining time and miles, if any, on the manufacturer's warranty.

You can also purchase a warranty at the time you purchase a used vehicle (or at any other time). You can buy a brand name extended warranty from a dealer, or you can buy a warranty from a warranty company. Be advised that many warranty companies have gone out of business, so you will want to get background information on any company from which you buy a warranty.

Bankrupt?

Do warranty companies really go bankrupt? That seems to be a widespread affliction. Joe had a warranty with a company that went bankrupt. Unfortunately, he didn't know it until he made a major claim (broken air conditioner). Fortunately, the dealership from which he had purchased the warranty (and used vehicle) made good on the claim, and he didn't lose money. But you can't count on such a happy ending.

Sources of Warranties

Warranties help sell vehicles, both new and used. Consequently, the warranty business is a big business. You shouldn't have any trouble getting a warranty for used vehicles that aren't too old or don't have high mileage.

Manufacturer's Warranties

You don't have to pay to assume a manufacturer's warranty. But make sure you fill out the requisite paperwork to let the manufacturer know you're the new owner.

Don't assume anything about a manufacturer's warranty. They vary greatly, and you must read the warranty to know what your coverage is. Indeed some manufacturers provide very thin coverage. You might decide that the manufacturer's warranty isn't worth much and that you need additional coverage from a warranty company. However, if you get a warranty or an extended warranty from a manufacturer, at least you probably won't have to worry about the company going out of business.

Warranty Companies

Warranty companies sell their warranties primarily through car dealers, because that's where the action is. Many will sell to you directly, though, via the Web or by telephone. If you buy direct, you're more likely get a good price.

Different warranty companies sell different coverage. Some provide few choices and others many choices. It pays to do some comparative shopping to find the coverage you want at a reasonable price.

Check out warranty companies carefully. One that's been in business for 40 years is probably more likely to be in business next month than one that's only been in business a year.

Dealer Warranties

Car dealers deal in warranties because warranties help sell vehicles. In fact, most warranties are sold through car dealers.

Short Term

Car dealers often provide short-term warranties on vehicles they sell. In fact, these are required by law in some state. These warranties are 30-day guarantees, 90-day guarantees, and the like. Usually you get something in writing in regard to these warranties, even if it's only one page. If you do get something in writing, review the document carefully to determine the scope of the coverage. If you don't get something in writing, you're never quite sure what you're getting.

Long Term

Dealers sell warranties. This is another cost in the hodgepodge of numbers you must track when negotiating with a dealer. You want to buy a warranty from the dealer at a competitive price. The dealer wants to make a big markup on selling you a warranty. Without a competitive price, you will be the loser in this game. If nothing else,

use 1Source (see below) to get a competitive bid any time you negotiate a warranty with a dealer.

One Way or Another

A dealer can get you one way or another if you don't do your
homework. Joe got a great deal on a used car once. But his wife
wanted a warranty. The dealer charged more than the going rate
for the warranty, and poor Joe couldn't do much about it due to
lack of information—even though he knew it was happening.

Dealers do not just sell manufacturer's warranties. They sell warranties provided by warranty companies as well. The fact that a dealer
sells warranties provided by a certain company is no guarantee that the
company won't go bankrupt. Don't rely upon a dealer to evaluate a
warranty company for you. Ask a lot of questions.

Certifications

Certifications aren't necessarily warranties. They are just a formal
statement that the vehicle operates and is in good repair at the time of
sale. The minute you drive a certified vehicle off the used vehicle lot,
you may be on your own. As a practical matter, many dealers also
include short-term guarantees or long-term warranties along with certifications. Check the terms of a certification guarantee or warranty to
see whether it provides adequate coverage for you.

For instance, with certification of Acuras, Acura dealers give an Acura
Care warranty. It extends the four-year and 50,000 mile manufacturer's warranty to a fifth year and 62,000 miles on everything, and to
seven years and 100,000 miles on the engine and drive train. For an
additional cost to the buyer, this warranty can also be expanded to
broader coverage.

Acura dealers can also provide similar certifications and warranties for
vehicles other than Acuras under their Easy Care and Primus Care

programs. Hey, this is a big business. Acura Care, Easy Care, and Primus Care are all underwritten by the Ford Motor Company.

Certifications with warranties are anything but uniform. Check the details to determine exactly what you're getting.

Coverage

What are you buying? Well, you need to buy coverage for a reasonable amount of time and number of miles. If you plan to keep the vehicle four years, you might want coverage for all four years. If you just want to make sure you're not getting a lemon, a year's coverage might be enough. Whatever you buy, you'll pay for it. In other words, four years coverage is more expensive than one year's coverage. Indeed, warranties are not cheap.

You may not be able to find coverage for old vehicles with high mileage. The warranty companies aren't crazy. Many warranty companies will not provide warranties on vehicles older than ten years. Until you inquire, however, you won't know what you can get.

Time Lapse

Buying a warranty with a maximum time period is for those who don't drive a lot of miles each year. If you are buying a warranty for 30,000 miles and you anticipate putting 18,000 miles on the vehicle each year, you need a two-year warranty, not a five year-warranty.

Mileage

Most people decide how many miles they want to insure and purchase a warranty accordingly. Thus, if you buy a vehicle with 40,000 miles and want to sell it at about 80,000 miles, it makes sense to get a warranty for 40,000 miles. It doesn't make sense to get a warranty for 60,000 miles.

Routine or Catastrophic?

In warranties there are generally two kinds of physical coverage. The minimal usually covers the engine, transmission, drive train, and suspension. The maximum covers almost everything. Of course, maximum coverage is more expensive.

Read Carefully

Read the warranty agreement carefully. Some warranties charge a deductible on every part used for a repair rather than just for the repair itself.

Generally, there two levels of deductibles, low and high. A low deductible might be $50. A high deductible might be $500. Of course, the low deductible is more expensive.

What should you choose? That's a matter of opinion. The authors recommend that you get maximum coverage with a high deductible. This amounts to catastrophic coverage and is reasonably priced. There are things that can go wrong with your vehicle other than the engine, transmission, drive train, and suspension that are expensive to repair (e.g., air conditioning). Why not cover them too? Paying for a low deductible, however, may not be cost effective.

First, with a low deductible you have to file a claim with every minor repair you get for your vehicle. That may be more trouble than it's worth. Second, it seems like most minor repairs are under $300. With $50 deductible (very expensive) you will cover 83 percent of the cost. With $100 deductible (expensive) you will cover 67 percent of the cost. It takes a lot of these repairs to justify the cost of a low deductible.

Major repairs range from $800 to $5,000. A high deductible will give you good protection to cover such expensive repairs without costing a fortune.

Most vehicles today are higher quality than 20 years ago, and there seems to be a general expectation that vehicles will go 100,000 miles with few minor repairs and no major repairs. In fact, many warranty companies will provide warranties only up to 100,000 miles.

Doesn't Cover Everything

Don't confuse what items warranties will cover. They don't cover normal replacements that are a part of routine maintenance such as spark plugs and cables, hoses, belts, brake pads, and the like.

Type of Vehicle

You won't get turned down for a warranty because you have the wrong vehicle, but you will pay a higher fee for some vehicles than others. One warranty company rates vehicles on a scale of 1-7. The #1 vehicles are the most reliable requiring the least repairs. The #7 vehicles are the most unreliable requiring the most repairs. Naturally, the owners of #7 vehicles pay more for their warranties than the owners of #1 vehicles.

Covered Components

Determine what's covered. Many warranty companies give you choices. You can get a minimal warranty that covers such basics are engine and drive train. Or, you can get a substantial warranty that covers almost all components in a vehicle.

1Source Warranties

Anyone can buy a 1Source (*http://www.1sourceautowarranty.com*) warranty for any purchase that meets 1Source's criteria. You don't have to purchase through eBay. Nonetheless, the fact that 1Source has a close relationship with eBay is, we hope, an indication that it probably won't go out of business tomorrow. See Figure 9.1.

1Source enables you can design a custom warranty (from a table) for your new used vehicle. Don't get too elaborate. The cost of warranties adds up fast. For 1Source or any other warranty company, read the fine print. Make sure you know what the warranty you are buying covers. See Chapter 5 for some ideas about what might go wrong with your vehicle and when.

Figure 9.1   The 1Source website.

Joe got a free quote online for a warranty for the 1999 Lincoln Town Car (see Chapter 3) with 50,000 miles. See Tables 9.1 and 9.2.

Table 9.1 Limited Coverage in Fall 2003

Term/ Mileage	Expiration Odometer	$0 Deductible	$100 Deductible	$200 Deductible
36/35,000	85,000	1,324	1,029	879
36/50,000	100,000	1,414	1,119	969
48/50,000	100,000	1,474	1,179	1,029
60/50,000	100,000	1,544	1,249	1,099
48/75,000	125,000	2,074	1,779	1,629

Coverage: Engine, transmission, drive train, fuel system, brakes, suspension, steering, cooling, air conditioning, and electrical. Specifically excluded are emission systems and high-tech components.

Table 9.2 Full Coverage in Fall 2003

Term/ Mileage	Expiration Odometer	$0 Deductible	$100 Deductible	$500 Deductible
36/35,000	85,000	1,624	1,329	1,029
36/50,000	100,000	1,734	1,439	1,139
48/50,000	100,000	1,814	1,519	1,219
60/50,000	100,000	1,894	1,599	1,299
48/75,000	125,000	2,574	2,279	1,979

Coverage: All components. Check the warranty agreement for specific inclusions and exclusions. This coverage is for breakdowns, not maintenance and routine replacements.

Check the 1 Source warranty agreement (available online) for specific inclusions and exclusions. Keep in mind, this coverage is for break-downs, not maintenance and routine replacements.

Don't Use These Numbers

The coverage and costs quoted above in the fall of 2003 are to be used for the purposes of illustration only and are for a specific car with specific characteristics. Don't use these numbers. They will not be accurate for your situation. Get your own free quote.

One catch is that 1Source warranties don't go into effect until after 30 days you purchase the vehicle (unless the new car warranty is still in effect). Consequently, the eBay free warranty (covered below) becomes an important benefit.

Components

1Source claims that its limited warranty covers about 600 components, and its full warranty covers about 4,000 components.

eBay's Warranty

eBay actually provides a warranty for no charge. It's for 30 days or 1,000 miles. You can look at it as sort of a bridge warranty. It will get you by until a purchased warranty from 1Source begins, but it's not a long-term solution. The eBay automatic free warranty does not extend to vehicles older than ten years or vehicles that have more than 100,000 miles. It's also a somewhat limited warranty.

Conclusion

We recommend that you get a full warranty with a high deductible. We also recommend that you negotiate the price with the dealer after getting comparative costs online (or offline). Be sure you know what's covered in your warranty and that the term and the mileage match your anticipated future use of the vehicle. Yes, we know that reading a warranty agreement is just one more tedious thing to do before closing, but it might cost you unanticipated thousands later if you don't read now.

10

Arranging Delivery

Arranging delivery fits in with completing the transaction. Once you're the owner, the vehicle is your responsibility. If you're in the seller's city, you can drive the vehicle home. Otherwise, you can have it stored or have it shipped. And, of course, always make sure it's insured (see Chapter 7) as soon as you become the owner.

Travel

Using the Web you can often find cheap airfares between major cities. It can be surprisingly inexpensive to fly to pick up your new used vehicle. However, it can be unduly expensive to fly if you or the vehicle are off the beaten track.

When you pick up a vehicle, you will have other expenses. You will have normal travel expenses during your travel by bus, train, or plane to reach the seller's city. On the way home you will have motel, food, and mileage expenses. Some states even charge you for driving across the state, because you won't have a permanent license for the vehicle (unless you bought the vehicle in your own state). All these expenses can add up fast if you don't plan well.

Referring to Chapter 3, you also have a mileage expense driving home. If your vehicle cost 42 cents per mile to operate and your city is 350 miles away, it will cost you $147 in vehicle expenses (including gas) to drive home.

Another consideration is what your time is worth. If given two extra days next week you can earn $125 per day, then a two-day trip to pick up a vehicle will cost you an additional $250. Of course it can be fun just to get out of town for a few days, and you can look upon a trip like this as a mini-vacation, not an expense.

Store and Travel

Often the sales transaction will come at an inopportune time. You may have to delay your travel to pick up the vehicle. Unfortunately, the storage problem is yours after you close the transaction. Most private owners will want your vehicle off their property as soon as possible. Some will insist that you remove it immediately. Even a dealer will not want to have your vehicle on the lot.

Therefore, it's up to you to negotiate storage into the deal if you cannot take immediate delivery. If you do this ahead of time, a seller may cheerfully (but secretly reluctantly) agree. If you try and negotiate storage after the deal is done, you will have a more difficult time making such arrangements. In any event, if you delay your travel long enough, you may have to arrange paid storage locally until you can pick up the vehicle.

Shipping

There are two ways to ship inside the US: by truck and by drive away. Both, of course, are very old and dependable businesses that give you alternatives to picking up your newly purchased vehicle yourself.

By Truck

Having a vehicle shipped is surprisingly inexpensive for long distances. It seems expensive, however, for short distances. Sometimes the seller can arrange shipping for you locally. Most of the time, however, you will make the arrangements. You have four choices:

1. Seller's address to your address

2. Seller's address to a truck terminal in your city

3. Truck terminal in seller's city to your address

4. Truck terminal in seller's city to a truck terminal in your city

Naturally, address to address is more expensive than terminal to terminal. Fortunately, you can estimate this cost online. eBay has an association with DAS (Dependable Auto Shippers - *http://dependableautoshippers.com*) that will provide you with a free quote online. Even if you don't use this company, a quote from them will give you a good idea of the cost (see Table 10.1).

Table 10.1 Typical Costs for Open and Enclosed Shipping via Truck

Atlanta to Albuquerque	Open Cost	Enclosed Cost
Terminal —>Address	$890	$1,195
Terminal —>Terminal	$740	$995
Address —>Address	$940	$1,295
Address —>Terminal	$890	$1,195

This quote for a specific vehicle was obtained in the fall of 2003 and will not be current by the time you read this. Note that shipping in enclosed trucks is more expensive than in open trucks.

More vehicle transport companies:

All States World Wide, *http://www.aswd.com*

All American Auto Transport, *http://www.aaat.com*

EzAutoShipping, *http://www.ezautoshipping.com*

For an even greater selection visit:

123 Movers, *http://www.123movers.com*

Ship Car Direct, *http://www.shipcardirect.com*

Drive Away

There are drive away companies such as Auto Drive Away (*http://www.autodriveawayla.com*) that will arrange for a driver to drive your vehicle home. A quote via the Internet for Atlanta to Albuquerque was $405 but did not include, of course, the cost of the miles put on the vehicle, which is not a factor with trucking. The driver is often someone unpaid recruited for a one-time mission, and the driver normally pays for gasoline. This is a reasonable and less expensive alternative to shipping by truck.

Delivery Cost

Naturally, you will want to investigate the cost of taking delivery before you purchase a vehicle on eBay. Local delivery is essentially free. Delivery from a distance city costs money. If you find a good deal on eBay and it still looks good after you add the cost of taking delivery, go for it. eBay offers plenty of good deals even after the cost of taking delivery is factored in.

Sellers Take Note

Generally speaking the cost of delivery affects the selling prices on eBay. eBay is a great marketplace for selling a vehicle, but expect the cost of delivery to lower selling prices.

Summary

You've got a problem when you buy a vehicle on eBay if you're a party to one of the 75 percent of transactions that takes place across state lines. That problem is getting the vehicle home. Perhaps the best, most inexpensive, and fun means of bringing home your purchase is to travel to the seller's location and drive the vehicle home yourself. Make a minivacation out of it. But shipping it home by truck is always an option, and that is reasonably inexpensive for long distances. Whatever you do, plan ahead and add the cost of transportation into the purchase price to make sure you're not overpaying to buy the vehicle.

III

Personal Selling

11

Selling Strategy

Need to get rid of a vehicle? Just put it up on eBay for auction, and you'll get a big hunk of cash for it. Ah, if only it were that easy. More realistically, to sell a vehicle on eBay, you need to develop a selling strategy. Or, if you don't like the work *strategy*, let's use the word *plan*. You need to develop a plan.

The first step in determining what to do is to read the Personal Buying section of this book. You need to see the buyer's point of view before you can be an effective seller. In addition, many issues and concerns that buyers face are identical to those that sellers face, and we can't

131

cover them redundantly in this book. Thus, the Personal Buying section of this book is just as much for sellers as for buyers.

Steps to Sell

Selling your vehicle successfully is a process that starts with a strategy and requires a series of tasks to be completed. It's not difficult, but it does take some effort.

To Fix or Not to Fix?

After you read the Personal Buying section, you need to make a decision about the vehicle. Sell it as is, or fix it before the sale? Either way you might sell it, but the trick is to maximize the money in your pocket at the end of the transaction. You will have to discount the price of the vehicle in order to sell it with an operational defect.

Some things are not worth fixing. Suppose you have an old vehicle worth $2,000. Are you going to replace the defective water pump at a cost of $390? Probably not. It's almost 20 percent of the value of the vehicle. There's likely to be a buyer who will buy it as is and replace the water pump himself. A water pump costs $90. The remainder is labor. Almost anyone with mechanical training can replacement a water pump. There's probably a buyer who with an appropriate discount will buy the vehicle and use his own labor to lower the purchase price.

Suppose you have a vehicle worth $12,000. Are you going to replace the defective water pump at a cost of $390 before sale? Probably. A person buying a $12,000 used vehicle doesn't want to be bothered with getting a water pump replaced immediately after purchase. He is looking for a good vehicle that's ready to roll.

Tires are always a consideration. Generally, we don't recommend replacing worn out tires, unless they are dangerous. The buyer might want different tires than you will buy. Instead offer a discount off the purchase price for replacing the tires. Or, be prepared to purchase new tires as part of a negotiated agreement. You can also give a cash rebate for purchasing tires. This will enable the new owner to get new tires and include them in her vehicle loan. In any event, good tires, whether actual tires or a cash equivalent, is an expected feature of a used car.

Read Chapter 21. You can purchase plenty of parts on eBay inexpensively to put your vehicle in prime condition. Many such parts you can replace yourself. Do you have a broken tail light? Purchase a replacement on eBay, use a screwdriver, and install it yourself.

Defects Inventory

You need to do a careful inventory of all the defects in the vehicle. Then you need to decide which ones you will fix and which ones you will pass on to the new owner. Of course, you will need to disclose the unrepaired defects in your sales pitch (the eBay ad in the eBay listing). That will give your sales pitch credibility and will avoid negative feedback.

Prepare for Sale

It's time consuming to get ready for a sale, and you need to make time in your schedule or pay someone else to do the various tasks. First you need to wash and wax the vehicle. Then you need to detail (clean thoroughly) the inside. Next you need to take photographs. There are services that will take care of these tasks if you can afford them. Finally, you need to take an inventory of defects as mentioned above.

If the vehicle needs repairs, you need to arrange for such repairs before you attempt to sell it, unless the repairs aren't justified due to the low value of the vehicle.

What about smog or safety tests? Does your state require them at the time of sale? If so, you need to get them done. Are you going to provide a mechanic's inspection report? If so, you need to arrange that.

Documents

Where are the vehicle documents? Do you have the vehicle title and other relevant papers you will need to close the transaction? If not, locate them before you offer the vehicle for sale. Otherwise you might be embarrassed when you can't provide the proper documentation to the buyer in a timely manner.

Do you know how to process the sale transaction (i.e., do the paperwork)? If not, you need to visit your DMV (department of motor vehicles) to learn. If you're a member of AAA (Automobile Association of America), they can help you.

Reports

What reports will you provide as part of your sales effort? As mentioned above, if you will provide a mechanic's inspection report, you need to arrange that. You can run a CARFAX (see Chapter 5) report yourself via the Web. Also run an appraisal on Edmunds (or Kelley or NADA – see Chapter 4) via the Web and include that in your sales information package. What about transportation? You might get some shipping quotes via the Web to sample cities to include in your eBay auction ad.

We recommend that you do all of the above and include the various reports in a sales package that you can deliver in print or electronically. The more information you provide, the better.

What if some of the information is detrimental to the potential sale? Our advice is to get it out in the open up front. That will save you a lot of problems and explanations later, and it will go a long ways toward preventing negative feedback.

Customer Service

Think about customer service. What can you offer potential buyers to make a purchase decision easy? How about: "Will deliver vehicle to any city within 300 miles of my home for no charge." What about 3,000 miles? This might make a good sales incentive and give you a chance to do some random traveling. Traveling to a random place (buyer's city) could be fun if you have the time. But there are a thousand other things you might offer or be ready to offer in regard to customer service.

A Sales Example

In 2000 Joe's 1987 Trooper ran well, and almost everything worked; but it had 200,000 miles and a body that looked drab. So, he thought he would sell it while it was still operational before a major breakdown occurred. He bought a 1995 Trooper and proceeded to sell the 1987 Trooper on eBay. The blue book value gave it a range of about $1,000–$3,500. He thought that he might sell it for $1,800. So, he started with a minimum bid of $1,400 and no reserve. It seemed that the only interest he would generate in such a vehicle would be local. Few people will travel to a faraway city to buy an old vehicle like this regardless of the price. In the case of his Trooper, something under $2,000 seemed about the right price.

Would he be able to sell this vehicle via an eBay auction?

After several family distractions (sick mother, Thanksgiving, and Christmas), he finally got around to preparing his Trooper for auction in January 2001.

He may have been able to get the Trooper to the eBay auction prior to January, except that he couldn't find the time to clean, polish, and photograph it. When he finally got around to doing the work, it took a whole day. Thus, he was able to include 11 good photographs in his auction ad. The auction resulted in one bid of $1,400. The buyer (430 miles away) was scheduled to pick up the Trooper on Friday the next week after the auction. Joe received a check for $1,400 that cleared. On the Thursday night before the buyer picked up the Trooper, Joe found out he had a problem with the title. It was lost. For a duplicate title, he had to get a release on a loan that was paid off eight years before. It would take a little time to get the release.

The buyer showed up about 5:30 PM on Friday to claim the Trooper. He was a pleasant middle-aged man who had driven into town with his elderly father in a late-model Lincoln. Before he looked at the Trooper, Joe explained the title problem to him. He said, "Fine." He asked no questions and signed the transfer papers. He walked away, got into the Trooper, and drove away without even looking it over. The entire transaction took less than five minutes.

Why did Joe not follow his own advice of going down to the DMV with the buyer to complete the transaction? There are two reasons. First, he did not have the title, so there was a question of how much he might have accomplished at the DMV. Second, it was after hours. The DMV wasn't open. This goes to show that there are practical considerations that sometimes interfere with standard practices. Note, however, that Joe did get the buyer's signature on all the proper documents, and Joe didn't cancel his auto insurance on the Trooper until after he sent the duplicate title and got acknowledgement of receipt. In California there is also a notice you send to DMV once a vehicle has been sold, and Joe also sent that before cancelling his insurance.

See Joe's actual eBay auction ad for the Trooper in Chapter 12, the next chapter.

Summary

Selling a vehicle on eBay requires organized effort to do a good job and get maximum bids. For many people, it's not worth the hassle. They would rather do a trade-in and let a dealer handle the sale. Would they do the same if they know they could save $1,000? $2,000? $3,000? Who knows? In any event, you can sell your vehicle and save what a dealer might earn, but to do it effectively requires planning. Develop a strategy to sell your vehicle, and then carry it through. It's likely to be much more effective than a haphazard effort. The used vehicle market is competitive, and you need every advantage you can create.

For information on additional marketplaces other than eBay, read Chapter 23.

12

Auction Listing

The auction listing is where the rubber meets the road, so to speak. There are over 200 Cadillac DeVilles on eBay as we write. For a prospective buyer, that's a skimming exercise. Don't interfere with that skimming. Make sure that all your title information is right to the point for the buyer-skimmer to find. In addition, make sure your auction ad is loaded with information.

Information Sells

The Internet is an informational medium unlike television, which is a hype medium (ads). You have unlimited space to tell the story of your product. And you need the space because the customer cannot walk up and fondle the product like in a showroom. Hype doesn't sell well on the Web.

Standard Information

This book continually stresses that information, not hype, sells merchandise on eBay. This is particularly important for big-ticket items such as vehicles. Provide prospective buyers with complete information on the vehicle that you auction. Include:

- Year, brand, and specific model
- Standard equipment
- Optional equipment
- Color
- Mileage
- VIN (Vehicle Identification Number)
- Detailed description of vehicle, including its condition and history
- Manufacturer's specifications (available from Edmunds)
- Good photographs from various angles
- Engine inspection report (to be provided upon request)
- Maintenance records (to be provided upon request)
- CARFAX Vehicle History Report (to be provided upon request)
- Edmunds appraisal (to be provided upon request)

- Boilerplate (standard information about payment and shipping)

- Customer service information

If you provide anything less, you will lose potential bidders for each item you omit. The ultimate result of leaving out information will be a lower winning bid.

Don't Waste Your Time

If you can't provide most of the information above, don't waste your time auctioning on eBay. You will be unlikely to have a successful auction. Attempt to sell your vehicle another way.

Engine Inspection Report

After an engine inspection, you can usually get an impressive printed report from corporate auto services such as Pep Boys. In fact, eBay has a deal with Pep Boys (in 36 states) to provide such reports for only $25.

AutoCheck Report

You can get an AutoCheck vehicle history report (one you can print) on eBay for only $5 or one from CARFAX for $10. See Chapter 5. You need the VIN to generate the report.

Appraisal Report

You can generate a presentable Edmunds (or Kelley or NADA) appraisal report free by going to the website and looking up the vehicle. You must have complete and accurate information on the vehicle to generate an accurate appraisal. As an alternative, suggest that prospective buyers go to the Edmunds (or Kelley or NADA) website and do the appraisal themselves. But you still have to provide them with complete information to enable them to generate accurate reports. See Chapter 4 for more information.

Posting the Reports

What do you do with these reports? You make them available. For instance, put them somewhere on the Web (in a digital form) where you can link to them from your auction ad. You can also print them to send to potential buyers who request them.

Bottom of the Ad

At the bottom of the ad you place standard information about handling the transaction, information about customer service, and photographs.

Boilerplate

This information is the same for every vehicle (i.e., every ad). You can use it over and over again. It instructs the buyer about payment and shipping.

Customer Service Information

The customer information can be part of the boilerplate if it remains the same for each item auctioned. Or, it can be custom information for each ad.

Photographs

Yes! Photographs are information too. Very important information. Photographs are essential for selling vehicles.

Non-Vehicle Ads

Ads for non-vehicles (e.g., auto parts) are constructed the same way. The only difference is that you may need to provide only one or two photographs for items that are not big-ticket items.

Titles Find the Items

Titles don't advertise. They help buyers find the auction ads that buyers seek. A title is limited by eBay to 55 characters. It goes into the head of the auction listing and makes up the one line entry in the lists of eBay auctions.

The title should clearly identify the item and should include searchable words appropriate for the item. Titles should be typeset in a normal manner. All caps, abbreviations, and jargon are taboo. Titles must be more than readable. They should be *easily skimable*.

Bad Example

WOW! PONTIAC GA 1997 WITH MR AND LOW MI L@@K!!!!!

Good Example

Pontiac Grand Am 1997 moon roof and low mileage

Note that the bad example is difficult to read quickly and impossible to skim quickly. Many people will not know what *GA* means. Many others won't know what *MR* means. Anyone using the search words *grand*, *am*, *moon*, or *roof* will miss the first title completely.

Bold titles and highlighted titles are available on eBay but are not necessarily more effective. Indeed, they are more difficult to read quickly and more difficult to skim. Naturally, eBay claims that bold titles and highlighted titles are more effective because eBay charges extra for them. Don't buy in.

Why don't we discuss the title first in this chapter? Because once you see that the real information is in the auction ad, you can understand that the title is simply the means for a buyer to identify an item (vehicle) in which she is interested. When she finds what she's looking for, she'll stop and read the ad.

Ad Layouts Display the Information

Prospective buyers find a vehicle via the title. Then they learn about the vehicle via your auction ad. Your ad needs to be presented in an easy-to-read format.

A Readable Format

The first rule of readability is good typesetting. Stay with the browser default (12-point Times New Roman or 12-point Times). Put the text in a column to make reading easy, about 400 to 500 pixels wide. Break the text in to paragraphs. Learn more about typesetting and layout in *eBay the Smart Way* Third Edition.

Start your text presentation with a summary heading that features benefits to users. (A little hype here is OK, so long as features are tied to benefits.) Then go into a full review of the product using good typesetting and good grammar. Stick to the facts.

For vehicles, don't worry about writing a good heading. Stick to the facts. People know a lot about vehicles, and they just want to know whether the vehicle they're reading about has what they want.

Sample Ad

The ad below is one Joe used successfully to sell his Trooper on eBay.

1987 Isuzu Trooper II S

4Dr – 4WD

Maroon

201,000 miles

VIN: JAACH14L7H6412895

2.3 4-cylinder engine, 5-speed manual transmission, power steering, power brakes, air conditioning, AM-FM cassette, almost new Firestone P235 75 R15 105S M/S Wilderness AT tires (replacements for the recalled Firestone Wilderness ATs), up-to-date maintenance.

Vehicle runs well. Everything works except:

- Left front parking light (white)

- Interior overhead light (works erratically)

- Backup lights (switch on transmission not working)

- Oil pressure gauge

- Light for LCD panel in AM-FM cassette player (clock)

Vehicle has a bent engine hood, which detracts from the appearance. The hood works OK. The front seats, while functional, are well worn.

Air conditioner runs well but not at its maximum as it has not been charged in over 6 years.

The engine burns oil. How much is difficult to tell because oil is apparently also leaking through a gasket. Oil loss is about 1 quart per 600 miles in normal driving, less on long highway trips.

Troopers are great off-road vehicles and fun and comfortable to drive otherwise too. Seller just purchased a 1995 Trooper.

This vehicle is ideal for someone in the San Francisco Bay Area or nearby who has a need for an old SUV that runs well.

Seller will split escrow fees with out-of-Area winning bidder. Carfax.com Lemon Report (http://www.carfax.com) will show clean title. Seller will also provide an emmissons report at sale as required by California law. You can do an appraisal at Kelley Blue Books (http://www.kbb.com).

Terms: Cashiers checks (or PayPal).

$200 deposit within 3 days. Remainder due on transfer of title within 10 days.

Bidders from Bay Area call to inspect before end of auction. Out-of-Area winning bidder can inspect after bidding is final.

Thanks for your interest.

Let's point out some things about this ad:

- The brand and model are clearly identified.

- The important information is at or near the top.

- The defects are listed in complete detail.

- The information ends on a positive note.

- Additional information in regard to handling the transaction is provided in boilerplate-like paragraphs. These paragraphs read like customer service, not like warnings.

This was not written by an advertising professional. This ad could be written by anyone. It's straightforward and factual. It was typeset in a readable column. The ad was followed by 11 photographs. Anyone interested in this vehicle had enough information to make a buying decision.

Is this a vehicle you want? Probably not. Nevertheless, there are buyers for this vehicle (and every vehicle) somewhere, and eBay is the best place to have a few of these buyers find you.

Use HTML

You can use HTML in your auction ad because the ad is in a webpage. The following HTML markups are the most useful for auction ads.

```
<p> [paragraph] </p>
```

This is the paragraph markup. It's very simple to use. Place one markup at the beginning of the paragraph and the other markup at the end.

```
<h3> [heading] </h3>
```

This is the heading markup. Place one markup at the beginning of the heading and the other markup at the end. The numbers 1 to 6 indicate the size of the heading with 1 being the largest. Use sizes 1 through 3. The remaining sizes are headings for small print.

```
<table width="450"><tr><td> [text] </td></
tr></table>
```

This is the table markup. Place one set of markups at the beginning of all the text and the other set of markups at the end of all the text. This makes a table (single column) 450 pixels wide, just right for browser default text.

You can read more about HTML in *eBay the Smart Way,* Third Edition, or read a basic HTML book like *Teach Yourself HTML & XHTML in 24 Hours,* Sixth Edition, Oliver and Morrison, SAMS, 2003. There are also many free online tutorials you can find using a search engine such as Google.

Template

A better way is to use an HTML (webpage) template like the ones you can find at *http://bookcenter.com.* You just copy and paste text right into the template.

Auction Management Service

You can use an auction management service to make your webpages. Such services invariably offer programming that uses templates to make attractive auction ads easily without knowing HTML.

Following the lead of the auction management services, eBay now offers auction management services including templates. Check out what eBay has to offer. It may be all you need.

The Worst

What's the worst you can do? Provide a lot of information without HTML formatting. If you enter text without paragraphing and without a column, you will get an unreadable block of text that spans across the entire listing webpage. It's amazing that people continue to do this on eBay, and it's also amazing the lack of bids they get as a result.

Listing Fee

The listing fees for vehicles on eBay Motors are not the same as for eBay. There is an initial insert fee of $40 for cars and other vehicles and $30 for motorcycles. There is no final value fee, but there is a transaction service fee (same as insert fee) at the time of the first bid or at the time of the first bid above the reserve where there is a reserve. These fees essentially consititue an advertising fee.

Note that the eBay Motors fees for Parts and Accessories are the same as the normal eBay fees.

Summary

The listing title gives you the best chance to help prospective buyers find the vehicle you are selling. Don't use it for advertising. Use it in a way that ensures buyers can find your vehicle. The eBay auction ad is your opportunity to provide all the information a prospective buyer needs to make a buying decision. Make good use of it. Provide plenty of information in a format that's readable and easy to use. And provide plenty of photographs.

Use this chapter as a guideline for ads in other marketplaces, too, such as the marketplaces covered in Chapter 23.

13

Photographs

Photographs enable a potential buyer to inspect a vehicle. Hey, a vehicle is a big-ticket item. Do you think someone is going to read the brand, model, year, and mileage and then rush to put in a bid and travel to a distant city to make an inspection? Won't happen. Photographs tell the story. Without photographs there is no story.

It is interesting that on eBay photographs sell merchandise well. Good photographs sell merchandise better. And great photographs do a superb job of selling merchandise. That photographs sell so well should not be so surprising. After all, in the offline world manufacturers spend a fortune on graphic advertising to sell new merchandise, and excellent photography is a prime element of graphic advertising. We're just amazed that if we do emulate the world of professional advertising as best we can, even as amateurs, it pays off.

The message here is that it's not enough to provide photographs. You need to provide good photographs of any vehicle you auction on eBay.

It's Work

Taking good photographs is more than just photography. It's work. First, you have to detail the vehicle. You have to clean it thoroughly inside and out. A waxing, whether manual or at a car wash, is necessary too. Your photographs should be good enough to display the vehicle in clear and colorful detail. If the photography is that good, then the vehicle needs to look pretty good. Hence, a detailed cleaning and polishing is important.

Second, you have to develop a plan to make good photographs. Sunny days don't make the best photographs. Dark overcast days make ominous unattractive photographs. You really need a lightly overcast day to make the best photographs. Depending on where you live, you might have to wait several days for tolerable conditions for shooting your photographs.

Third, you have to make time to take photographs. For instance, you need a good shot from every angle. Inconveniently, when you shoot photographs from every angle, you'll end up shooting into the sun on almost half your shots. That doesn't work very well. So, you will probably need to move the vehicle several times during your shooting session just to get the sun falling from the proper direction onto the side of the vehicle you're shooting. This is a concern even on lightly overcast days.

In addition, you need to shoot the vehicle in a proper setting. Photographing a luxury car with a dilapidated industrial background is better than nothing, but it doesn't make good advertising. It would be better to shoot such a vehicle in a nice residential neighborhood. Shooting a vehicle inside a building with florescent lighting without the proper film or without the proper white balance (for digital cameras) will result in photographs with an unattractive color cast to them.

By the time you clean and prepare the vehicle, shoot the photographs, get all your vehicle records together, research price information on the Internet and on eBay, and enter your auction ad on eBay, you've done a good day's work. A good part of that is the cleaning and photographing.

Vehicle Photography

Vehicle photography is an art and takes a huge amount of expertise. How can you hope to duplicate professional photographs of vehicles? You can't. But you can still do a good job that shows three important things:

1. What the vehicle is. If you're selling a Chrysler Town & Country van, buyers need to know what it is. They may be looking for a van, but they may not know what a Town & Country is until they see the photograph.

2. The vehicle's condition. A buyer wants to know exactly what condition the vehicle is in. One thing (e.g., a small inconspicuous dent in the door) may bother some people but won't bother others. Some things are a deal killer. Others aren't. Until a buyer sees the defects large or small, however, neither you nor the buyer will know whether the vehicle is acceptable to the buyer.

3. That the vehicle looks good. New vehicles look great, even if they're utiltiy vehicles or even if they're models you don't like. There's something about a nice clean polished look that does wonders for the appearance and appeal of any vehicle. You want

to show in your photographs that the vehicle you are selling can look good. You do that by showing via photographs that the vehicle does, in fact, look good. That's why it's important to wash and polish your vehicle before you take the photographs.

Photo Tips

The following photo tips will help you take better pictures.

1. Take photographs on a lightly overcast day. Second best is a sunny day but in the open shade. Third best is on a sunny day making sure the sun is behind you for all your shots. Fourth best is inside with multiple photo flood lights. Fifth best is inside with an adequate flash.

2. Watch what's in the background. You don't want it to be something distracting, ugly, or unpleasant.

3. Fill the frame with the vehicle. When the vehicle is only two-thirds of the photograph or less, it's difficult to adequately capture the detail you need.

4. Use a tripod and focus carefully. Tripods help ensure that your photographs will be sharp.

5. Take at least twice as many photographs as you intend to use. More is better.

If we were going to recommend that you use film, we would list a few more tips. But we're not going to do so. We strongly recommend that you use a digital camera. Why?

- You can check a photograph instantly to make sure the photograph is a good one.

- You can shoot lots of photographs without worrying about loading another roll of film or worrying about the cost of processing.

- You can use your photographs instantly for an eBay Motors auction.

- You can manipulate your photographs easily using widely-available digital image editors to make the photographs look great.

You will need a minimum of a 2-megapixel camera now available for under $80. We feel this is a small price to pay for getting good photographs (instantly available) for a big ticket item. If you're a tightwad, buy a used digital camera on eBay, use it to take your vehicle photographs, and then sell it on eBay after you're done. It's cheaper than renting.

The alternative is to use film and then get the photographs digitized somehow. One way or another, you need to come up with multiple photographs to sell a vehicle on eBay for the highest possible price.

Picture CD

One inexpensive way to digitize your film photographs is to order a Kodak Picture CD with your photo processing.

Indeed, we believe it's practically impossible to sell a normal vehicle on eBay without providing at least one good photograph. But the more, the better. Look at dealer auctions on eBay. They always include at least a few good photographs, and they're the expert sellers.

Take a photograph from every angle: front, back, right side, and left side. Shoot the inside through the driver's side door, from the rear (van or SUV), and at the dashboard. The photographs should be clear and sharp. Also photograph every noticeable blemish.

Close-Up Photography

To shoot the small defects in a vehicle may require close-up photography. With a film camera you may need a macro lens to get usable shots. One of the useful aspects of digital cameras, however, is that they take great close-up shots without a macro lens.

Seeing photographs is the primary way a potential buyer has of making a purchase decision. If you ignore this fact, you eliminate many potential buyers and make yourself look like an eBay rookie.

Image Editing

Use an image editor to doctor your photographs (see Figure 13.1). Image editing software comes bundled with PCs, digital cameras, PC video cards, and other hardware and software. You may have on on your PC already. Look for software with "photo" or "paint" in the name. You can download a popular image editor called IrfanView free at *http://www.irfanview.com*. See Figure 13.2.

Figure 13.1   IrfanView image editor.

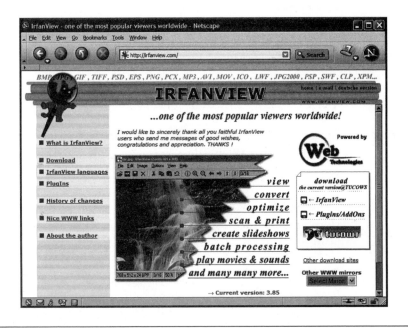

Figure 13.2   IrfanView website.

Darkroom

An image editor is a digital dark room. In fact, it's the equivalent of a very expensive physical darkroom. You can manipulate an image in a wide range of ways if you have the photographic knowledge to do so. For our purposes, however, there are just a few simple things to do.

Crop

As mentioned above, you want the vehicle to fill the frame. If you take a good photograph that you want to use where the vehicle doesn't fill the frame, you can crop away the excess. You can also crop a small defect (that you want to show) out of a larger photograph to make a close-up.

Brightness

You can change the brightness. For instance, you can make a dark photograph brighter. Interestingly, you can darken most photographs a little, which together with increased contrast makes a richer and sharper photograph.

Contrast

Increasing the contrast makes photographs look sharper. Use together with decreasing the brightness to give a photograph a rich look.

Sharpness

Sometimes all you need to do to get great photographs is to use a sharpening control in an image editor. However, if you change the brightness and contrast too, do the sharpening last.

Resize

Finally, you need to resize the photograph to the size you will use in your eBay auction ad. Normally photographs no wider that 400 pixels are best for eBay ads. But vehicles are big-ticket items. Someone looking for a vehicle will wait longer for photographs to download than they will when looking at a $20 item. Therefore, you can use larger photographs than normal. Nevertheless, don't use digital photographs wider than 600 pixels.

You can use the image HTML markup *<img src=" " width=" " height=" ">* to resize the photograph. Suppose you use a photograph 1,200 x 800 pixels. You can use the image markup to resize it to 600 x 400 by using the *width* and *height* attributes of the image markup. However, the entire 1,200 x 800 image must download. It's much better to resize a copy of the original photograph to 600 x 400. It will take a lot less time to download.

Aspect Ratio

When you resize, always maintain the aspect ratio, the ratio of the width to the height. If you don't, the photograph will become distorted.

Visual Evaluation

There are no magic formulas for processing digital photographs. Experiment with your image editor and use what looks good. Using the controls mentioned above, you can process your photographs quickly and easily.

For more detailed information on photography for eBay items, read *eBay the Smart Way* Third Editon or *eBay Business the Smart Way*.

Photography Service

There's a new photography service available for eBay vehicle sellers. Check out Auction 123 (*http://www.auction123.com*). See Figure 13.3. They will send someone out to photograph the vehicle you intend to sell and then provide you with a nice multi-photo presentation for your auction ad. And it's not too expensive: $50 for dealers and $65 for individuals. This service will invariably produce better photographs than doing the photography yourself (unless you're an accomplished photographer). And they do the auction listing for you as well as the photographs. The listing ad includes many color photographs nicely displayed.

There are also other photography services primarily aimed at dealers. Often photography services are associated with a listing service to provide a complete online service for dealers. Try DiamondLot, *http://www.diamondlot.com*, for dealers services that include photographs. Dealer Specialties, *http://www.dealerspecialties.com*, provides similar services.

Figure 13.3   Auction 123 website. ©2002-2003 Auction123 Inc.

Summary

Photography is crucial to selling vehicles on eBay Motors. The more photographs, the better. The better the photographs, the greater the number of bidders, thus the higher the sales price. It's worth your time to give attention to taking the best photographs you can and include them in your auction ad.

14

Customer Service

For those of you new to online commerce, customer service is the name of the game. Online sellers have to compete with offline retail sales. Offline merchants (including used vehicle dealers) have a substantial advantage. They are where the customers are. Customers can come in and fondle the merchandise and after a quick purchase can take immediate possession of the item purchased. When selling online, how can you compete with such convenience?

The answer is that you can give superb customer service. Now, we all know that in spite of the convenience of shopping locally, superb customer service is no longer a hallmark of the American retail industry most places offline. But online it's a different story. Online shoppers expect and get excellent customer service for online sellers (vendors), at least from the ones that are still in business. If you want to sell effectively, expect to go that extra mile for your customers.

Selling on eBay Motors is no exception to online customers' expectations of good customer service. The big question is, How does the customer service idea translate into selling vehicles?

Address the Needs of the Buyer

The obvious answer to that question is to address the needs of the buyer. But such a reply begs the question. The real question is, How do you satisfy the needs of the buyer? We don't have all the answers. In fact, the used vehicle market online is just in its infancy, and there are many customer services yet to be invented. All we can offer is a proper attitude and a few examples.

Empathize

Your first task as a seller is to read the portions of this book, or otherwise do research, to understand what the poor buyer has to do to purchase a vehicle on eBay. First, she has to make a buying decision based on photographs and written information. Then she has to win the auction committing herself to a purchase sight unseen. Then she has to travel to a distant city to take delivery of the vehicle. In many cases she has to trust an ill-informed person like herself to document the transaction properly. Hey, how much can we ask of one person? You've got to have empathy.

Present a Good Attitude

You have to be friendly. Now, this is tough for many sellers, particularly dealers. Why? There are coteries of young hawbucks out there who just bid on auctions for the fun of it without any intent to buy the items. eBay Motors is one of their favorite playgrounds. They make dealers and other sellers quite angry.

So, sellers have auction ads with dire warnings and rules about how to respond to their auctions. Of course, it doesn't bother the hawbucks but rather just encourages their digital vandalism. And it leaves the rest of us friendly, hardworking, no-nonsense folks wondering what's going on. Some sellers have bad attitudes—very common on eBay— where good attitudes are required for maximum success.

When you're selling anything, the customers are your friends. When you're selling big-ticket items, such as vehicles, the customers are your cherished friends. If you start out with a bad attitude, you won't get a chance to develop the credibility you need to sell your vehicle successfully.

Start out with a good attitude, a friendly attitude. Your auction ad should reflect your friendly attitude. Love your potential buyers. Good things will flow from your friendly attitude.

Non-Paying Bidders

As for those playing auction games, eBay has instituted programs to cut back the non-paying bidder (NPB) traffic. Normal hard-working folks are getting tired of hackers, NPBs, and others of such ilk. In the future, we can expect harsher penalties for such miscreants both on eBay and in the criminal justice system.

Provide Complete Information

Providing complete information isn't just a marketing technique. It's also a customer service technique. Complete information includes all basic information on the vehicle together with a complete and accurate description of the condition of the vehicle. Don't shortchange your potential buyers. Give them everything.

Keep in mind, of course, that you may be able to use other Internet sources to provide information. For instance, for vehicle specifications you may be able to provide a link to a manufacturer's website or to another website where vehicle specifications are archived.

And don't forget photographs. Photographs are important information. They are particularly important to potential buyers of vehicles.

Take advantage of services like Edmunds and AutoCheck. Generate reports, post them on the Web, and include links in your auction ad to such reports. Make it easy for people to make a decision.

Be Accommodating

You have to read this together with Chapter 15 regarding your personal security. But here we will make the case for making it convenient for a buyer to come to your city to evaluate and take delivery of the vehicle.

Contingent Inspections

Allow contingent sales. That is, allow a sale contingent on financing, a visual inspection, a test drive, and a mechanics inspection. The worst that can happen is that the buyer backs out of the deal. But how likely is that? If a buyer commits to traveling your city at his own expense, the buyer is serious about buying the vehicle, and you should accord him the same courtesies that you would a local buyer.

Visual Inspection and Test Drive

A visual inspection and a test drive are done by the buyer. They should be done as soon as the buyer gets to town. If he finds something that's going to kill the deal, it's better to know sooner than later.

Mechanic's Inspection

Many buyers will also want to take the vehicle for a mechanic's inspection. Many service stations will give priority to such inspections, and you can usually get one done in a short time. As a seller, you need to know of several such places nearby so you can make a recommendation to the buyer. Get an understanding, of course, that the inspection is at the buyer's expense.

Keep in mind that an eBay buyer who can inspect, test drive, and have the vehicle inspected by a mechanic *after the auction* will take less risk in the purchase and will be willing to bid higher.

One way to decrease the buyer's desire for a mechanic's inspection is to have the vehicle fully inspected yourself before offering it for sale. Don't take it to your local favorite mechanic. Take it to a service center (with a corporate name) that issues a detailed computer-generated report. For high-mileage vehicles, make sure the report includes manual compression tests on each engine cylinder or a comparable test. Make xerox copies of the report to send to prospective buyers. The report must be recent to have credibility. This will satisfy many prospective buyers, but not all.

Scanned Reports

You can also scan reports, post them on the Web as photographs, and link to them in your auction ad.

Note that eBay has made an arrangement with PepBoys, a national chain of auto service centers, to do an inspection for $25. These inspections come with an impressive computer report, but they don't include a compression check.

Repairs

You may want to sell a vehicle that needs repairs for which you are not going to pay. Try selling the vehicle at a discounted price instead of making the repairs. Perhaps the buyer will find something in disrepair that you did not disclose, in which case you are obligated to repair it at your expense. In either case, the buyer may want to have the repairs made before he drives the vehicle out of town. In the meanwhile, he has no transportation. See the Be a Travel Agent subsection next.

Be a Travel Agent

Again, read this together with Chapter 15 on security. We will make the case here that you should help the buyer visit your city. The buyer will need a ride from the airport, train station, or bus depot to the place of the vehicle inspection and then perhaps to a motel. The buyer may want recommendations for transportation to your city, for a motel, and even for a restaurant. And the buyer may need additional local transportation during the time repairs, if any, are being made to the vehicle. Provide a map of the city to assist the buyer to get around and eventually leave town. You don't have to go overboard, but you get the idea. The buyer is not your guest, but he is a guest in your city; and you represent the city, in effect.

Tend to the Documentation

As the seller, you need to take the lead on making sure the proper documentation is signed to consumate the purchase transaction. Since the vehicle is in your possession and in your state, it is most convenient for you to do the paperwork.

In most cases the buyer will be from out of state, and you will need to obtain—or get the information on how to obtain—a temporary license for the vehicle. The buyer will drive the vehicle to his state and get a permanent license there.

The best practice is to go to the DMV together with the buyer to turn in the paperwork and pay whatever fees are appropriate. However, in many cases the lending institutions involved (your lender or the buyer's lender) will either give you guidance for doing the documentation or most likely will do it for you.

Have the Vehicle Ready

You cleaned and polished the vehicle for photographs. When the buyer arrives to take delivery, you probably won't have much work to do to get the vehicle in top condition. Nonetheless, do make sure the vehicle is clean and polished when the buyer takes delivery. This is just common courtesy.

For Dealers

Develop a strategy and a routine for handling eBay buyers. Use some of the ideas in this chapter, and develop some ideas of your own. Avoid publishing unfriendly warnings and conditions in your eBay ad. Where such warnings and conditions are required by law, publish them with some visual separation from the rest of the text and label them as a *Statutory Notification*. Forget about the non-paying bidders. You aren't going to scare them off. Let eBay develop the means to control them.

Used car dealers have a reputation for acting aggressive, overbearing, and disregardful of customer concerns (although certainly most are not that way). It's difficult to use such behavior effectively via email and telephone. In addition, the commercial culture online has developed into one where customer service has a high value. This challenges good salespeople to use less forceful sales techniques online and to develop new ways to sell vehicles, particularly on eBay.

Summary

Customer service is all-important on the Web and particularly important for big ticket items such as vehicles. It is especially important on eBay Motors. This is one aspect of selling for which you don't want to cut corners. If you're a dealer, it will make you or break you on eBay.

IV

Concerns for Both Buyers and Sellers

15

Security

Security has two aspects: the security of the transaction and your personal physical security. This chapter explores these aspects for both buyers and sellers. The security of the transaction is important because there are many vehicle scams coming down the road. You need to be viglilant. Your physical security will probably be fine, just by using common sense. Nonetheless, you have to be careful to protect yourself against those rare individuals who might do you harm.

Reputation

eBay's feedback system is especially important for buyers and sellers at eBay Motors for several reasons:

1. A vehicle is a big-ticket item.

2. The transaction has many components, all of which need to be handled so as to satisfy both the buyer and seller.

3. There's a substantial likelihood of meeting the other party in person.

4. The seller's generous customer service is indispensable to a successful transaction.

No careful person would go into this kind of a transaction without trusting the other party. eBay provides that trust through the eBay feedback system. Consequently, our advice to you for vehicle transactions is to deal only with those people whose feedback makes you feel comfortable. Don't take a chance.

Non-Performing Bidders

Some eBay bidders make a winning bid just for the fun of it, with no intention of completing a purchase transaction. As a seller, it's tough to protect yourself against such people who abuse the system. Treat them like non-performing bidders (NPBs) in any other eBay auction. Give them negative feedback.

These miscreant bidders pose an unfortunate threat to vehicle sellers. Many people who sell a vehicle have already purchased their replacement vehicle. They own two vehicles at once with double loan payments and double insurance payments. They don't want to waste time selling their old vehicle. Winning bidders who don't perform can cost sellers money in this situation.

Likewise, NPBs pose a threat to honest bidders. An honest bidder must go to a lot of trouble to get ready to bid (e.g., line up financing and insurance). To get beat out by a NPB just wastes their time and effort.

Don't Go Overboard

As a seller, however, you shouldn't go overboard to protect yourself against NPBs. Simply require a payment (e.g., $500) within a short time (e.g., two days) to flush out the phonies. Make the remainder of your purchasing process buyer-friendly. Someone who makes a good-faith payment and then travels to your city to inspect the vehicle is not likely to be a phony.

Verification

To bid more than $15,000 on eBay, you have to either put your credit card on file or go through the ID Verify process. This is something to note because many vehicles will cost more than $15,000. This assures eBay and the seller that the bidder is a known person, not someone fraudulently hiding behind an alias and playing bidding games.

Life is a two-way street, however, and buyers might consider requiring that the seller go through the ID Verify process. It's the buyer who incurs the financial risk of an incomplete transaction. Suppose you travel from Memphis to Omaha to pick up the vehicle only to find that the seller doesn't really own it. He's selling it for a friend and has represented himself as being his friend. And suddenly his friend changes his mind about doing the deal. You've just made a trip to Omaha for naught. Hence, if a seller doesn't have ID Verify, you might consider passing and moving on to another vehicle.

In our opinion, ID Verify should be a basic requirement for participation in eBay as either a buyer or seller for transactions that exceed a reasonable amount (e.g., $500). Due to the dollar size of a vehicle sale and the financial risk that a buyer takes in traveling to pick up the vehicle, ID Verify should be mandatory for both buyers and sellers participating in eBay Motors. eBay is remiss in not requiring ID Verify of both.

eBay and PayPal do, however, impose some verification requirements on sellers for sales over threshold amounts. These requirements for both buyers and sellers are changing. Bring yourself up to date on the latest requirements via the eBay website and be aware of your own status (this reflects on your credibility) and the status of the other party.

ID Verifiy

The ID Verify costs you about $5 (one time only) and verifies to eBay and the world that you are who you say you are. The ID Verify is easy and convenient to obtain.

Eliminate the Phonies

Requiring ID Verify for all winning bidders on eBay Motors will eliminate a lot of NPBs who have no intention of completing a purchase. Unfortunately, the verification process is seen by many as something sinister or unjustified. Thus, a requirement to be verified with a low threshold price might significantly reduce the number of legitimate eBay participants.

BuySafe

The Hartford, an old line insurance company, now offers the BuySafe program (*http://www.buysafe.com*) wherein sellers can become bonded. That provides real security to buyers. At one percent, it's not cheap for sellers, but a buyer will feel much more secure buying from a seller that has the BuySafe seal in the auction ad. Essentially, it means that buyers will be reimbursed if they don't get what they pay for.

Joe is in favor of having bonding be made a requirement for all eBay Motors sellers. Alas, that is unlikely to happen soon. Nonetheless, it seems probable that the day will come sooner or later when bonding will be required of all big ticket eBay sellers. It will all be part of the maturing of this new and huge online marketplace.

Agency

An agency relationship is one in which one party acts legally for another party.

Buyers

As a buyer, in some cases you will find that the seller doesn't really own the vehicle. He is selling it for someone else. If you suspect that an agency exists, ask questions. In fact, ask anyway. Before you take a plane from Denver to Baltimore as the winning bidder to pick up the vehicle, you need to make sure that the auction is binding on the seller. The only way to do so is to get a copy of the agency agreement between the true owner of the vehicle and the person who auctioned it on eBay.

Don't Take the Risk

For a Isuzu Trooper on which Joe bid via eBay, this very problem came up. It is common for vehicles to be auctioned on eBay by people who are not the owners. Most of these formal or informal agencies will not be a problem. You don't want to take the risk, however, of traveling to a distant city to find that the true owner doesn't want to sell for the winning bid and is not legally bound because a valid agency agreement doesn't exist. Or, you don't want to find that the vehicle has been sold by the true owner to someone else. So, ask for a copy of the agency agreement before you venture to the distant city.

Sellers

A concern about agency isn't as crucial for sellers. At worst, you will waste your time if you are dealing with an agent instead of the true buyer and the deal does not close. Agency buying is widespread (e.g., a husband buying a car for his wife). There's not a lot you can do about it. Just remember that there are certain legal practices you must follow (e.g., disclosures) and certain signatures you must get to engineer a successful sale. If the true buyer is out of the picture and the agent is calling all the shots, you still have bring the true buyer into the picture enough to meet the legal requirements of the transaction and to provide the proper signatures.

Mediation

You can ask the other party to agree to mediation in regard to disputes that may arise from an auction transaction. SquareTrade, the eBay recommended service, is a great way to do this inexpensively and effectively. Purchasing a vehicle involves a large financial transaction. It's well worth it to have the most complete protection possible; mediation through an organization like SquareTrade can provide you with assurance that you will get treated fairly. In fact, SquareTrade thinks of itself as a type of insurance.

Sight Unseen

Some buyers seem willing to take more risks than others. They will buy a vehicle, not inspect it, and have it shipped to them from afar. This seems kind of crazy. But it might not be as crazy as it seems. Assuming that the vehicle has not been fraudulently misrepresented by the seller, what's the worst case for the buyer?

The buyer should not buy the vehicle in the first place if the shipping cost plus the purchase price exceeds the retail value. Therefore, at worst, the buyer will have a vehicle that he or she doesn't want but nonetheless one that was purchased at retail value or below. The buyer should be able to sell the unwanted vehicle in his or her local market or on eBay. Thus, the entire process can often yield only a reasonably small loss or even a wash financially. Unfortunately, the sales tax is an ever present burden but usually not a disaster.

I don't advocate that you make a purchase this way, but in certain circumstances it may be worth the risk. The more difficult it is to find the vehicle you want, the more likely you will be to take risks as a buyer when you do find your dream vehicle.

Phony Online Escrows

Beware of phony online escrow companies. They take your money and disappear. Try to have the transaction handled by a dealer or a bank. In any event, check up on any companies that you don't know. Go to SOS 4 Auctions (*http://www.sos4auctions.com*) to find legitimate escrow companies.

eBay Local Purchase?

Can you do a local purchase on eBay? Certainly. If a seller in your city sells your dream vehicle on eBay, it makes things simple for you. Treat such a purchase like any local purchase. You can insist on the proper protections covered in this chapter, and you're present to act in an expeditious manner to complete the transaction. Indeed, many eBay vehicle transactions are local transactions.

Personal Security

Personal security is an issue any time you do business with strangers, particularly in situations and places unfamiliar to you. Most people will ignore what we say here and take risks in dealing with strangers, because it's more convenient than minimizing risks. Indeed, we don't insist that you follow our suggestions here, as we sometimes don't follow our own guidelines. Nevertheless, we include this section for people who are concerned with personal security. You can't go through life sanely and be paranoid, but it pays to be aware and to use commonsense.

Buyer's Situation

You don't have a personal security problem so long as you have the vehicle shipped to your home. If you travel to a distant city, however, you need to stay aware. In a distant city you will be alone, probably without friends, and about to meet a complete stranger to take delivery of your vehicle. What can you to do to protect yourself? This question becomes particularly significant when that complete stranger will pick you up at the airport or train station in a car.

Unfortunately, we can't answer this question definitively. You need to use commonsense. Nonetheless, there are a few precautions you might take.

1. Know the telephone number and physical address (not PO Box number) of the seller. Test the telephone and address, if practical, to make sure they're real.

2. Make sure someone at home has this information. Let someone know what you are doing, where you are going, who you are dealing with, and when you expect to get back.

3. Take one other person with you if practical.

4. Provide your own transportation once you get to the distant city. Don't rely on the seller. Renting a car will make it easier to follow these precautions.

5. Meet the seller in a public place (e.g. Starbucks).

6. Insist on doing the test drive by yourself. Insist on taking the vehicle for a mechanic's inspection by yourself.

7. Take delivery in a public place (e.g., DMV).

8. Make use of a cell phone in creative ways to insure your security (e.g., give someone back home a periodic report on what you're doing). You may not be able to count on cell phone service everywhere, however, outside of large cities, so take that into

consideration when going to remote places.

Fortunately, if you buy from a dealer, you won't have to be quite as cautious. Just show up at the dealership showroom and work from there.

The New Dealers

There are a group of dealers who do business only on eBay. They keep an inventory of vehicles not on a used car lot with a show-room but in a warehouse that could be anywhere since no public access is required. You might want to be be a little more cautious about meeting the seller at an obscure warehouse than at a more public place of business.

Seller's Situation

A buyer will want to inspect and test drive the vehicle. Meet the prospective buyer in a public place, not at your home. Dealing with strangers at your home may not be advisable.

Local Buyer

Locally, you will have trouble selling a vehicle to an intelligent buyer without allowing a test drive and an engine inspection. Ideally, you will take someone with you to meet the prospective buyer in a public place (e.g., Starbucks) to allow the inspection.

Before allowing a test drive, politely require that the prospective buyer produce a driver's license. Note the name and driver's license number. As a seller, you should go on the test drive. If you do go on the test drive, agree with the prospective buyer where you will go and what time you will be back. Leave the person who came with you at the public place (together with the prospective buyer's driver's license number).

You may not want to go on the test drive with a stranger. Don't go if you don't feel comfortable. Let the prospective buyer go alone.

Many prospective buyers will show up for the test drive with their spouse or a friend. Some may show up with several friends. If you feel threatened by the extra people, decline the test drive and leave.

Take Precautions

We don't intend to over caution you on the risk of meeting someone who will do you harm in regard to a vehicle sale. The chances of that are slim. Nonetheless, when dealing with strangers, take common sense precautions and stay alert.

eBay Buyer

You have to extend more courtesies to out-of-town buyers and perhaps take more risks. Nonetheless, with an out-of-town buyer, you should have written information on the person. Leave a copy with a friend or relative.

Allow an eBay winning bidder the same inspections you would allow a local prospective buyer. Why wouldn't you? Follow exactly the same procedures. Your personal risk is perhaps lower because a stranger from out of town is probably less likely to be a threat.

Keep in mind that a prospective eBay buyer who can inspect and test drive the vehicle and have the engine inspected on a contingent purchase after the auction will take less risk in the purchase and will be willing to pay a higher purchase price.

Customer Service

Good customer service dictates that you provide the courtesy of picking up a buyer at the airport or train station, facilitate a test drive and inspection, and complete the transaction. Sometimes you may even have to drive the buyer to a motel because you can't close the transaction until the next business day.

Then too, you need to be aware of security and develop creative ways to minimize your personal risk. Following a procedure like that suggested for buyers may be helpful.

1. Know the telephone number and physical address (no PO Box numbers) of the buyer. Test the telephone and address to make sure they're real.

2. Make sure someone at home has the buyer's information. Let someone know what you are doing, where you are going, who you are dealing with, and when you expect to get back.

3. Take one other person with you if practical.

4. Meet the buyer in a public place (e.g. Starbucks).

5. Make use of a cell phone in a creative way to insure your security.

As you can see, customer service and security can be conflicting concerns. You need to strike a balance with which you feel comfortable.

At the Bank

If there is a loan to be made or paid off at a local bank in regard to the transaction, that bank is a good place to meet to complete the transaction. Banks will normally provide a conference room (or other room) for bank customers for such use.

Dealer Sellers

If you are a dealer-seller or a salesperson, make your place of business (i.e., your used car lot and showroom) the location for your dealings with the buyer. That will make both you and the buyer feel more secure.

Summary

Both the security of the transaction and your personal security are at issue in an eBay vehicle transaction. Make sure the other party is the person he claims to be. If he's the seller, make sure he's the actual owner of the vehicle. And keep in mind that the eBay feedback system provides you with dependable reputation information. As for your personal security, stay alert and use your common sense.

16

Negotiation

Although the auction and fixed-prices are supposed to take all the negotiation out of a transaction, it doesn't work that way for vehicles. Vehicle transactions have lots of components, and not all of the components get priced on eBay. Consequently, if you can negotiate well, you can make a better deal for yourself. Keep in mind, too, that making the deal better for yourself doesn't necessarily mean making the deal worse for the other party (although sometimes it does).

Call and Buy

If you use the process discussed in Chapter 8 where you call the seller and attempt to negotiate a deal, you work outside eBay. In this situation, you negotiate everything. See a list of negotiable items in the Negotiate Separately subsection below.

Buyers & Sellers

This section is for both buyers and sellers. Later in the chapter there are separate sections for buyers and sellers.

Know the Value

The best auctioning technique, the best sales technique, and the best negotiation technique is to *know the value* of the vehicle. Sometimes you can appraise a vehicle easily. Sometimes it requires a lot of research. But it remains the best buying or selling technique of all.

Love the Vehicle

Loving the vehicle is an essential ingredient for successful negotiations for both buyers and sellers.

Seller's Love

As a seller, you have to love the vehicle. Otherwise, how can you build the enthusiasm it takes to make a sale? If you just can't love the vehicle for some reason, at least learn to stress the positives and downplay the negatives (although you need to fully disclose any defects).

Have empathy for buyers. You may not be able to love the vehicle yourself, but you can love the idea that it's suitable for the buyer; and that will generate the enthusiasm you need to make the sale. That will make you love the vehicle.

Suppose you're stuck with selling your daughter's Honda Civic. She just left for a year of college abroad in Spain and doesn't need it any longer. You don't like foreign cars. Nonetheless, you can empathize with a potential buyer who is a young woman like your daughter and who needs a reliable inexpensive car that gets good gas mileage. No vehicle is right for everyone, but every vehicle is right for someone.

Love must be sincere, however, to be effective. If you try to fake it, most people will see through you. If you can't bring yourself to love the vehicle or if you can't love the idea of the vehicle being perfect for someone else, then perhaps you should let an agent sell the vehicle for you.

Buyer's Love

As a buyer you have to love the vehicle. Many buyers believe it's a good negotiation technique to feign dislike of the very vehicle they want to buy. Make the seller work hard to talk you into a purchase, and you'll get a better price, right?

Actually, this doesn't work well. You're more likely to turn off the seller and make him think he shouldn't waste much time with you. The better approach is to be honest. If you find something you like, be enthusiastic about it. Saying you love the vehicle draws in the seller and builds the foundation for some serious negotiations. When complications arise in the negotiations—as they often do—the seller will stick with you. In short, the seller will try harder to make the deal if you love the vehicle.

Lay a Solid Foundation

People don't negotiate and make deals enthusiastically with people they don't trust. One of the basic steps toward a successful negotiation is to build a rapport with the other party. This takes honesty, courtesy, consideration, friendliness, fairness, and other behaviors that build trust. This starts with the first contact with the other party and continues throughout. The most successful negotiation is one to which the parties commit themselves because they trust each other.

Note that loving the vehicle is part of laying a solid foundation, too, an essential part that you should not overlook.

Make the Deal by Telephone

This is the digital age, and you can do any kind of business via email, right? Alas, if life were only that simple. The truth is that every means of communication has its place. And email definitely has only a limited role in negotiation. It is best to negotiate face to face. But that's not possible when doing business via eBay and the Internet. Consequently, negotiating via telephone is the next best means. Email just doesn't work well.

Email can be a harsh medium of communication, even for good writers. Email is best used to convey hard information such as names, addresses, vehicle serial numbers, forms, reports, and the like. It is a poor medium for the subtle nuances and the ongoing give and take of communicating to put a deal together.

That is not to say that email cannot play an important role in buying and selling vehicles. Certainly, it's very handy. But when the going gets tough, you better get on the telephone, or else you will lose the deal.

In Person

Negotiating in person is better than negotiating over the telephone. Unfortunately, in many eBay transactions negotiating in person is not practical.

Listen Carefully

Always listen carefully. Even if you get into an argument with the other party (not advised), take turns talking and listen when you're not talking.

The buyer and seller must each get what they need out of a transaction, or the transaction is unlikely to be completed. Sometimes the other party either isn't clear about what they want or doesn't know what they want. If you listen carefully, you may be able to figure it out and then lead the other party into an agreement that satisfies everyone.

A great way to listen is to keep your mouth shut for extended periods of time. Not easy!

Follow Up

Always do what you say you will do. That is, follow up. If you tell the other party that you will send a document tomorrow via Federal Express. Do it. It's all part of building trust and laying a solid foundation for the completion of the transaction. No follow-up task is too small or insignificant after you've promised the other party that you will do it.

Ask

A famous real estate lecturer from Oregon used to say, "Ask not, and you shall receive not." The moral of the story is that if you want something, ask for it. A surprising numbers of times you will get what you ask for. Don't be so sure that the other party is going to say "no" that you miss a lot of opportunities. Let the other party decide for himself after you make the request.

The same lecturer also said, "Don't tell me what you won't do. Tell me what you will do." Who cares what the other party won't do to reach an agreement. It's irrelevant. What's relevant is what they will do. Hence, it's important to keep discussions going in a positive direction by asking questions that elicit positive answers.

Compromise

It kills negotiation to be rigid and uncompromising. Americans love compromise. Nonetheless, don't be afraid to stick close to your initial offer. If you don't want to compromise much on the price, find something else on which to compromise. Make only small incremental price changes in your offers (or counteroffers).

Keep It Going

Never close negotiations by simply refusing an offer. Always make a counteroffer. Be creative. Likewise never close negotiations by letting the other party simply refuse your offer. Make another offer.

Split the Difference

Splitting the difference is a time-honored American negotiating technique. It's very compelling because it's fair, right? Unfortunately, it's only fair in a limited number of situations. Otherwise it can be a trap. Don't fall for it.

Suppose you're selling a Ford van. You research the price and find it to be $18,250 retail and $15,100 wholesale. Your goal is to sell it for $16,500, and you set the price at $17,100.

A potential buyer comes along and makes you an offer of $9,500. Not wanting to close off the negotiation, you make a counteroffer of $17,000. Then the buyers comes back and makes another offer of $10,000. You counter with $16,900. Then the buyer comes back and says, "Let's make it fair, let's split the difference." That would indicate a sales price of $13,450. Is that a fair price? Hardly. A fair price is presumably somewhere between wholesale and retail.

On the other hand, suppose you are negotiating with a buyer, and he makes his third offer at $15,500. You make your third counteroffer at $16,800. He comes back and says "Let's make it fair, let's split the difference." That would indicate a sales price of $16,150. Is that a fair price? Sure. Is it an offer you should take? Maybe. It doesn't reach your goal of $16,500, but if you're tired of negotiating, it's an offer you might take. Nonetheless, if you're determined to reach your goal of $16,500, you might agree with the buyer that splitting the difference is fair, but that it's fairer for him than for you. And you're not willing to do it. Hold out for $16,500.

Splitting the difference is most effective—and perhaps most fair—when the parties have negotiated to a point where the distance between their latest offer and counteroffer is small.

Don't Lose Your Temper

The other party's point of view is valid even if it doesn't match your point of view. The objective is not to annihilate the other party's point of view. Rather, it is to reach an agreement. And don't get frustrated if the other party tries to annihilate your point of view. Your point of view is well researched and well supported by fact. You don't need to become alarmed. Always remain calm, friendly, and open-minded.

If you find yourself losing your temper, or if the other party starts to lose his temper, a good idea is to adjourn the negotiation until the next day giving both parties a chance to cool off.

Don't Rush

Don't be quick to accept the other party's offer or counteroffer. Always say you need to check something (e.g., talk with your spouse) first. Make it seem like you have to consider the seller's offer carefully even though you're secretly eager to agree immediately. This is just good psychology. Otherwise the other party may come to think they have made a mistake and offered too much. Such an attitude may endanger the transaction.

Always Get It in Writing

Always reduce your agreement with the other party to writing. The best way is to use a standard vehicle purchase and sale contract from the state where the vehicle is owned. Get a copy from a stationary store, a dealer, or a state website. Get it signed as soon as possible after you've agreed verbally.

Build Your Confidence

The best way to be confident in your negotiations is to know the value of the vehicle. You know that the sales price will be close to the market value if both you and the other party negotiate with any skill at all. So, market knowledge can't help but build your confidence.

In addition, with a little brainstorming, you can come up with some creative offers and counteroffers. With confidence in your creativity you can easily feel that it's quite likely you will be able to make a deal in any reasonable situation.

If you have confidence in yourself, the other party is more likely to have confidence in you, and that will make reaching an agreement easier.

Buyers

There are a few negotiating techniques just for buyers. This section covers a few of them.

Negotiate Separately

Let's take a look of a list of things that might be sold to the buyer by a dealer:

1. Vehicle

2. Financing

3. Warranty

4. Insurance

5. Shipping

6. Reconditioning or repairs

7. Special Work

The best way for a buyer to negotiate is to negotiate each item separately. Why? Because you can find the information to ascertain the price of each item. That's particularly easy to do on the Web, where you can find appropriate pricing resources.

Once you let everything be lumped together in one general negotiation, you invariably lose track of the individual components. This gives the dealer a distinct advantage. Remember dealers negotiate car sales everyday. Everyday! They have a genius for making generous profits on the components of the sale. If they don't get you on the price of the vehicle, they will nickel and dime you to death on the other components.

Remember, dealers offer a host of services in-house. For instance, they don't have to go anywhere to get you financing for your purchase. They can write the loan right on the desk in front of you. They get a spread on the interest and a premium for originating the loan. It's not unusual for a dealer to make more profit on the lending than on the vehicle.

Look carefully at the list. The only item for which eBay sets the price is the vehicle. Everything else is up for grabs. Make sure you are either providing everything else from your own sources or at least know the competitive price of every component.

Welcome Dealers

If you have confidence in your negotiation capabilities, don't be afraid of a dealer. Dealers are always realistic even when they're blowing smoke at you. You can make your best deals when the other party is realistic. But you have to work at it. A dealer isn't going to give anything away without something of a struggle. Hang in there, have some fun negotiating, and you will make a deal.

On the other hand, negotiating with an unrealistic private seller is often a waste of time. Unfortunately, a surprising number of sellers fall into this category, at least during the first month of trying to sell their vehicles. With published values for used vehicles on the Web, there are not as many unrealistic sellers as there once were, but there are still plenty to go around.

Make an Offer

Don't be afraid to make a reasonable offer. With research you can find out the market value of any vehicle. Don't be afraid to make an offer near market value.

For example, suppose you find a low-mileage red Volvo S70 for sale for $16,900. It's a cool vehicle for which you've been looking for four weeks. You do your pricing research and find the retail price to be $13,250. Your goal is to buy it at $1,000 under retail ($12,250). This is a reasonable goal and a price point where you've got a good chance to make a deal. What do you offer?

Don't be afraid to offer $11,750. This will give you a little wiggle room if the seller takes an interest in your offer. But you're $5,150 under the seller's asking price! So, what! That's the seller's problem, not yours.

By the way, this is not a lowball offer. Suppose the wholesale price for this vehicle is $10,500. We would consider an offer to be a lowball offer only if the offer were under $10,500 (i.e. under wholesale).

Make One-Time Offers

You can make any offer you want to on any vehicle. If you make take-it-or-leave-it lowball offers on every vehicle you can find that meets your requirements, you will take a long time to buy your next vehicle. But that's OK. That can be a good strategy if you're a penny pincher and have patience.

What you're really doing is looking for a distress sale. You're looking for someone who desperately needs to sell their vehicle now, today, at any price. If you make enough offers, sooner or later you will find someone who will sell a good vehicle to you at your lowball price.

If this is your strategy, stick to it. Don't get sidetracked by a seller who wants to negotiate. You will usually end up wasting your time or paying more than you want to.

Keep in mind, however, that this is a special strategy. Most of us don't have the time or energy to carry through this strategy. We would rather pay more, buy a vehicle sooner, and get on with our lives.

Sellers

Two of the negotiating techniques just for sellers are included in this section.

Be Straight

Don't misrepresent the facts. It may kill the deal sooner or later. At worst, it will result in negative feedback for you. Just tell it like it is. For instance, disclosing defects in a vehicle actually builds confidence in the negotiations.

You don't have to misrepresent the facts. There are buyers for vehicles on eBay regardless of the condition of the vehicle. It's a huge marketplace.

Don't Over Price

Price high and negotiate down to a price where you can make a deal, right? Not exactly. High prices scare off a significant percentage of the buyers. They will think you're unrealistic and will waste their time.

Always price a vehicle close to market value and then maintain your negotiating position. The reasonable price will draw buyers but will not prevent you from sticking close to your asking price.

The eBay Milieu

How does negotiation enter into the eBay setting? Don't eBay auctions set the prices of the vehicles? There are two answers to this. First, as discussed, the price of the vehicle is only one component of the total price. The prices of the other components have to be negotiated. This is especially true when the seller is a dealer.

Second, as discussed, many buyers are making successful offers off eBay to sellers to preempt other eBay buyers or because they were never on eBay in the first place. Again, this is especially true when the seller is a dealer. Read more discussion on this in Chapter 8.

Consequently, you may find yourself negotiating more often than not when you attempt to buy or sell a vehicle on eBay.

Summary

Everyone has their favorite negotiating techniques. Many books have been written about negotiation. And we have included a few techniques in this chapter that we think will help you make a deal. Put it all together and make a deal.

Think through your negotiations well before they start, develop a strategy, and commence negotiating with confidence.

Negotiation isn't just for cars and trucks or just for eBay. It works for all motor vehicles and all marketplaces. When you read Chapters 22 and 23, keep this negotiation chapter in mind.

17

Completing the Transaction

It's the story of paperwork and payments. Completing the transaction is a tribute to bureaucracy; that is, *tribute* not in the sense of an acknowledgement of esteem but in the sense of an exacted contribution of documents and money. It's almost worth getting a loan to own a vehicle just because the financial institution will take care of most of the paperwork and the payments. If there's not a financial institution or dealer involved, however, you're on your own to complete the proper paperwork.

Safe for Buyers

eBay recognizes that doing a deal on a vehicle with someone in another city whom you've never met is risky. So, eBay has arranged the following aids to help you ensure a secure purchase.

Limited Warranty

eBay offers each buyer a limited warranty for 30 days on vehicles less than 10 years old with under 100,000 miles. It's free. But it's also quite limited. It works nicely with other warranty programs that require a 30-day waiting period before starting. Read more about warranties in Chapter 9.

Purchase Insurance

eBay also offers purchase insurance at no charge. If you, as a buyer, end up with a vehicle that is substantially less than represented, then eBay will pay damages so long as the damages amount to more than half the purchase price. Again, this is quite limited coverage. But it's better than nothing. However, this insurance also covers extreme cases where:

- You don't receive the vehicle or title.
- The vehicle was stolen at the time of the transaction.
- There was an undisclosed lien against the title.

Read the coverage statement to get the full details.

PayPal Deposit

A deposit for the transaction can be made through PayPal. This provides the normal protections for both buyers and sellers that are built into PayPal. The seller must be willing to use it.

Secure Pay

Secure Pay is an escrow-like arrangement offered by Escrow.com and featured by eBay Motors. It's an easy and inexpensive way to make payment secure for buyers. The seller must agree to use it.

Seller Guarantee

This is similar to the purchase insurance program, although the coverage is less. It's designed primarily to resolve disputes between buyers and legitimate sellers that have to do with the disclosures about the vehicle. The seller has to specifically qualify for and join this program before it is available to buyers.

Others

All of the above are on the eBay Motors website. In addition, we've already discussed the eBay Pep Boys vehicle inspection program, AutoCheck vehicle history reports, and other protections for buyers. Together, all of these services arranged or provided by eBay constitute a safety net established for a buyer's convenience. Using these services on eBay may amount to a safer approach for a buyer to successfully complete a transaction than the way buyers do it in the offline world.

Closing

To complete the transaction, go with the other party to the Department of Motor Vehicles (DMV), or whatever it's called in that state, to complete the transfer of ownership and to fill out and sign all the paperwork. Make sure all the seller's liens are removed from the title and that the title is free and clear. The buyer pays sales tax and vehicle registration fees in her home state. If the buyer purchases out of state, she will pay only small transaction and temporary registration fees and no sales tax. Going through the transfer process at the DMV is your only assurance that everything gets done correctly.

Contact the DMV ahead of time to determine what is required to to complete a transaction. The DMV Online website lists URLs for all the state DMVs (see also Appendix IV).

http://www.onlinedmv.com/index.html

If you're the buyer, always make sure you check the VIN (Vehicle Identification Number) of the vehicle against the VIN on the title. Otherwise you may find yourself very embarrassed at some point in the future. Don't forget to have your car insurance in place prior to the transfer of ownership. You are liable for your newly purchased vehicle.

Buyers Check for Salvage Title

Always check with the DMV to determine if the title is a salvage title. You can do this at the DMV if you close at the DMV. A better idea is to do it over the phone well before the closing. Online reports such as CARFAX do not always catch a salvage title.

After Hours

If you will close when the DMV is not opened, you need to be more prepared. You should go to the DMV ahead of time and get the necessary documents. Have the DMV help you make a checklist of things to do (e.g., documents to get signed) in the closing.

AAA

If one of the parties is a member of the AAA (Automobile Association of America), the AAA may handle the closing. In some states the AAA is authorized to act for the DMV and handle vehicle paperwork. Exactly the extend of what the AAA can do will vary from state to state. But the parties almost certainly will have to show up at an AAA office to close this way.

Escrow

You may need to set up the transaction in escrow if:

You cannot be present in the distant city when the transfer of ownership takes place; or

There is a lender lien on the title (the seller owes money on the vehicle); or

You are borrowing from a lender to make the purchase.

The escrow is extra paperwork that is sometimes expensive to arrange, but it may be necessary.

Escrow Scam

Look out for phony escrow companies. The con artist seller runs the phony escrow website. The buyer wires the money into escrow, and the seller disappears with the buyer's money and the car (if there actually was a car). You can use Escrow.com safely. Check out all other escrow companies carefully whether online or offline. Use a bank or reputable dealer whenever possible.

Use SOS 4 Auctions (*http://www.sos4auctions.com*), a website that lists fraudulent online escrows companies, to check up on an escrow company. It lists legitimate companies too. Also, visit the National Consumers League website for tips on choosing an escrow company (*http://www.nclnet.org/shoppingonline/escrowtips.htm*).

Escrow.com

For a one percent fee, Escrow.com (*http://www.escrow.com*) will provide an escrow transaction. It will verify payment for the seller, and it will withhold payment from the seller until the buyer has inspected the vehicle and is satisfied. Although the fee seems reasonable, as the book went to press, this service was inadequate for many situations. For instance, it did not handle loan payoffs.

Take a look specifically at Secure Pay, an escrow-like program set up by Escrow.com especially for eBay Motors. It's an easy and inexpesive way to get escrow-like protection.

Bank Escrow

An escrow agreement is particularly valuable when the seller still owes funds to a lender on the vehicle, and he or she will use your purchase money to pay off the loan. The escrow is your only assurance that the seller's loan gets paid off.

Perhaps the best place to arrange the escrow in the case of a loan payoff is the seller's lender. The seller's bank can adroitly handle the transaction because it can pay off the seller's loan instantly with the buyer's purchase payment.

Informal Escrow

Most lenders will do informal escrow arrangements. Rather than using a formal escrow agreement, for instance, a buyer's lender might accept an executed bill of sale and title from the seller. In return, the lender will give the seller a letter stating that the seller will receive a check for the purchase price as soon as the paperwork for the buyer's loan transaction is complete. When two lenders (seller's and buyer's) are involved, you can expect them to work out the details of completing the transaction, often without a formal escrow agreement. Even with a lender and a dealer, the transaction will move ahead smoothly without a formal escrow agreement.

Let the escrow agent worry about the transfer details. But the buyer shouldn't overlook the problem of taking responsibility for the vehicle immediately after the transaction is complete. The escrow agent isn't going to put the vehicle in her garage until the buyer gets to town if the buyer happens to be buying from a distant city.

TitleTransfers.com

Try this dot com company to handle the transfer documents. It might make your transaction easier and smoother, particularly when there is not a lender or dealer involved on either the buyer or seller side. However, understand that this is not necessarily an escrow arrangement and does not provide all the protections of an escrow arrangement.

Escrow Fee

An escrow arrangement is so germane to an eBay vehicle transaction which involves a seller's loan payoff that the escrow fee should be split. Indeed, this is true for most eBay vehicle transactions except where the seller can provide clear title and the buyer and seller can go to the DMV together to complete the transaction. eBay is not going to dictate the terms of agreement for a transaction, but as a practical matter and as a matter of fairness, the buyer and seller should split the escrow fee. Ask the seller to do so prior to the conclusion of the auction.

Dealer

Dealers do vehicle transactions every day as part of their business role. If the seller is a dealer, leave the details of the transaction to the dealer-seller and don't worry about an escrow arrangement.

Dishonest Dealers

When I say you can rely on dealers to take care of the details of the transaction, I am referring to most licensed car dealers. They can be expected to take care of the paperwork properly. But there are always a few dishonest ones around, so proceed with caution. Make sure you are dealing with a reputable dealer.

Don't Assume

If you are the seller, don't assume that because the buyer has paid for the vehicle that he or she will carry through on the paperwork, such as getting a new title. Buyers have many reasons why they don't get around to registering the transaction and officially taking title. One of the primary reasons is that they must pay sales tax when they officially take title to the vehicle.

Suppose a buyer sits on the paperwork and does nothing. As the seller, you still have your name on the title. If anything happens with that vehicle (e.g., an accident), you may be liable.

Therefore, walk buyers through the closing transaction at the DMV and make sure they have title to the vehicle before you bow out of the picture. Otherwise you might find yourself faced with a legal claim based on the fact that you're still the owner of record for the vehicle.

Mail-In Forms

Some states, such as California, have a mail-in transfer report that the seller can send to the DMV after the transfer to report the transfer. As the seller, make sure you mail this to the DMV after the transfer, if you didn't do the transfer at the DMV. And don't cancel your insurance until you're sure the DMV has the paperwork.

Documents & Fees

There are various documents and fees that are a part of a vehicle sale transaction. Use this section as a guide to make sure you have all the bases covered.

Auction

When the auction is complete, the parties are legally bound to complete the transfer of title for the vehicle for the price of the winning bid, unless they subsequently agree not to do so. All states have reasonably similar laws regulating auctions, and if you fail to perform according to the terms of the auction, you will be liable to the other party. Consequently, the auction itself may become the purchase agreement between the parties.

Don't forget to keep a printed copy of the auction ad and all the other eBay documents for your records. Include eBay emails and also emails between you and the other party. You may need them.

Parties

You would think the seller was the owner of the vehicle and the buyer (bidder) was to be the new owner. That's not necessarily the case. Husbands get on eBay to auction their wives' vehicles; friends get on eBay to auctions their friends' vehicles; and even agents get on eBay to auction their clients' vehicles. It's the same for buyers. These casual agencies are common on eBay. You don't know who the owner is until you ask. Likewise, you don't know who the new owner will be until you ask.

Agencies can be dangerous. Suppose you agree to auction your friend's car that he hasn't been able to sell in three months. You successfully auction it for $6,500 under your own eBay ID ($200 more than his bottom price). Right after the auction someone local offers your friend $7,500 for the car, and he accepts. You are left holding the bag. You can't deliver the car to the eBay buyer, and you will almost certainly get negative feedback. In addition, you are liable to the buyer.

If you are operating under an agency agreement, make sure it's written. It probably won't make much difference in regard to feedback, but you will be able to bring your nasty friend into the law suit should you get sued.

Purchase Agreement

If you enter a purchase agreement outside the auction, make sure it's a written agreement. There are miscommunications and misunderstandings, and written documents seem to avoid such mishaps more than oral agreements. If practical, use a standard form agreement from the state where the vehicle is licensed and titled. You can get a standard form from a dealer, a stationary store, or perhaps at the DMV.

If the auction is completed but you change the terms of the agreement after the auction, put the new agreement into a written purchase agreement.

Title

The title is usually in the state where the vehicle is licensed, but not always. Sometimes a person moves from one state to another neglecting to transfer the title to the new state. In any event, the title must be signed by the owner to effect a transfer. The title is the most important document. If the title isn't transferred, the buyer may have nothing.

If there is a loan on the vehicle with an unpaid balance, the lender usually has possession of the title. If you want to auction your vehicle on eBay, make sure you know where the title is before you list the vehicle. If you can't deliver the title in a timely manner, you are sure to get negative feedback.

Release of Lien

If a lender has a lien on the vehicle to secure a loan, the lien usually appears on the title. In order to make a transfer free and clear of the loan, you have to pay off the loan. When you do, make sure the lender signs the release of lien on the title.

Bureaucratic Fees and Documents

There are sometimes special documents, minor fees, disclosures, and the like that may be required by some states in regard to the transfer of a vehicle. Make sure you know what they are and comply.

For instance, in California, you must have a recent smog certificate any time a vehicle is transferred. The report goes from the service station that performs the smog test right to the DMV electronically. The DMV gets the paperwork, and the buyer pays the service station for the smog test. The seller can have the smog test completed ahead of time as long as it is not more than 30 days before the transfer takes place; it might help the seller to sell the vehicle, but ultimately it is the buyer's obligation.

License Fee

The annual license fee for the vehicle is paid to the state where the buyer lives and the license plates are issued. If the buyer is from out of state, the seller doesn't have to worry about that. If the buyer is in the seller's state, the parties should present the entire transaction to the DMV all at once, which will require a check from the buyer made out to the DMV for the annual license fee.

Note that the annual license fee is substantial in some states and nominal in others. This can be a major expense. Don't be surprised.

Sales Tax

One cannot license a newly-purchased vehicle without paying the sales tax first in the state in which the vehicle will be licensed. If the buyer is from out of state, the seller doesn't have to worry about that. If the buyer is in the same state as the seller, the parties should present the entire transaction to the DMV all at once, which will require a check from the buyer made out to the state treasurer for the sales tax.

Again, note that sales tax is a major expense in many states. In California it's about 8 percent. That means that on a $20,000 vehicle, the sales tax will be $1,600. This is not a detail you should overlook until the closing.

Temporary License

If the buyer is not in the same state as the seller, he will have to get a temporary license for a minor fee. This is usually a 30-day or 60-day permit (not a license plate). The seller should arrange to get this permit for the buyer, which will enable the buyer to legally drive home. The seller should not leave his license plates on the vehicle.

If the buyer is in the seller's state, the license plates may transfer with the vehicle. Check with your DMV about this. If the plates don't transfer, the buyer may need a temporary permit. Again, check with the DMV.

Checks

All checks to pay fees and to make payments should be cashier's checks. If you use personal checks, it opens up possibilities for fraud or at least for bounced checks. Checks issued by the bank from a special account or by the dealer handling the transaction are OK too.

Case Study

Joe was going to start looking for a larger car than his wife's 1994 Mercury Sable, which his wife no longer trusted. (It was one of Ford's well-known great engineering disasters and not dependable. Even several attempts to sell it on eBay at a rock bottom price failed. But that's another story.) Joe and his wife wanted a large car, something heavier and presumably safer than a standard-size car. He ran across a 1989 Cadillac DeVille with 74,000 miles at a weekend sell-it-yourself car mart in early 2001. It was in perfect condition with a low price, and he bought it on the spot. He and his wife were not Cadillac people, but the low price converted them.

This purchase moved Joe to look at Cadillac DeVilles on eBay just out of curiosity. He found about 135, some at bargain prices. He began to see that luxury could be a permanent and inexpensive option for him and his wife.

The Cadillac turned out to be a nice car. Darn nice. In the fall of 2003 at 105,000 miles, a noise developed in the engine, which broke the bond of trust between his wife and the car. It was time to find another car.

Naturally, Joe turned to the DeVilles on eBay. By this time there were almost 300. Lots of bargains. Many seemed to be a long distance away from the San Francisco Bay Area (e.g., Florida), however, and he decided to look at other large cars, too, such as the Buick Park Avenue, Ford Crown Victoria, Mercury Grand Marquis, and Lincoln Town Car. There were again many bargains available. He found a 1999 Town Car with 49,000 miles in perfect condition in Eugene, Oregon, not too far away from home.

Unfortunately, he couldn't bid on it immediately. This was to be his wife's car financed through her credit union. She hadn't talked to the credit union yet and wanted to check with them before bidding. He emailed the seller Bob Rose, a salesman, that he was interested but couldn't bid yet. The bidding was over before Joe's wife had a chance to talk with her credit union, but the bidding had not reached the reserve. Consequently, Joe emailed Bob after the auction and after his wife's talk with the credit union that they wanted to purchase the Town Car. Bob said that he would sell it to them. Then Joe ran an AutoCheck check, and the report showed no problems.

Luckily, there didn't seem to be any competition to purchase this car. Bob offered the Town Car to Joe at $11,250, about $2,500 under wholesale value. Since Joe usually seeks to buy at wholesale value or a little above, Joe didn't negotiate. He just accepted the offer contingent on financing, a mechanic's inspection, and his own inspection. The seller was a leasing company, which employed Bob, and had apparently taken the car back after a customer defaulted on a lease.

Although Joe expected to take a bus to Eugene (flying was too round-about), he found that Amtrak had a daily train scheduled. Thus, he rode the train to Eugene. The last four hours between Klamath Falls and Eugene the train runs through a beautiful mountain wilderness, a real treat.

Joe arrived in Eugene on a Sunday. Bob picked him up at the train station, and they went to Bob's office to work on the deal. Joe couldn't get the car to a mechanic until Monday morning, but he and Bob got everything else done. For instance, as a dealer Bob was able to issue an Oregon temporary permit for the vehicle. Joe gave Bob possession of the check from the credit union, and Bob gave Joe possession of the car. But the deal was still contingent on the mechanic's inspection. Now Joe was in Eugene with a beautiful Lincoln Town Car.

There was one little glitch. Joe wanted this to be an eBay transaction specifically to get the free 30-day warranty. He ordered a 1Source warranty, but it didn't start until 30 days later. So, Bob put the Town Car back on eBay at a fixed price, and a minute later Joe purchased it.

A Little Bizarre

This exercise of making this deal an eBay deal to get the 30-day warranty was a little bizarre. Bob didn't own the car (the leasing company did), and Joe didn't buy the car (his wife did). Yet the deal was between Bob and Joe on eBay. What were these guys thinking? The answer is, they weren't.

Monday morning Joe took the car in for a mechanic's inspection, which took about an hour. It checked out OK except for two minor things that didn't work and about which Joe already had knowledge. Bob had authorized Joe to get them fixed at Bob's cost, but the mechanic would not do so without a scheduled appointment. As a result, Bob and Joe negotiated a cash settlement based on the estimated cost of repairs. At 10:30 AM Monday Joe was on his way home. Very nice car. Good price.

The moral of the story is that between the credit union and the leasing company, which was a licensed auto dealer, all the paperwork was done professionally, and the transaction closing went smoothly with little effort on Joe's part.

Vehicle Price?

Let's get sidetracked for a minute. Why was the price of this Lincoln so low? First, the color was powder blue with white leather upholstery. This is an attractive combination for a woman but is otherwise difficult to sell. Second, the leasing company had the car on its used car lot for several months due to the lack of employing a salesperson specifically to sell used cars. They hired Bob only a few weeks before this deal was made. Bob's job was to sell off inventory as fast as possible. Bob, who already had experience selling cars on eBay, turned to eBay to help get the job done. Joe and his wife got lucky.

Bob sells a lot of vehicles locally in Eugene, presumably at prices above and below retail. But he says every time he is authorized to sell a used vehicle at wholesale price or below, he auctions it on eBay. Even at wholesale, he says he makes a sale on only about one car out of three vehicles auctioned on eBay.

We must assume that Bob's experience is not unusual. That means that a lot of vehicles listed on eBay can be purchased at wholesale prices. For buyers, that's a lot of good deals just waiting for you.

Summary

Every vehicle purchase is different. There's no such thing as a normal transaction. Yet people buy vehicles everyday making such purchases commonplace. Buying a vehicle on eBay is not mysterious or even unusual. It's just a commonplace purchase. If there's a lender or dealer (or both) involved in the transaction, the deal will likely be closed in an informal escrow-like process wherein the lender or dealer takes care of the paperwork.

Otherwise, it's up to the parties to close the transaction by themselves. Perhaps the best way to do so is in a joint appearance at the DMV (see Appendix IV for a list) to make sure all the paperwork is done properly and all requisite fees are paid. At the very least, consult with the DMV to make a closing check list that ensures that you do everything correctly and use the proper documents.

V

Dealer Selling

18

The eBay Way

eBay has its ways. It has a tradition. It has a community. And it has a reputation system called "Feedback." eBay presents used vehicle dealers with a wonderful new market in which to sell vehicles. It's not a fad. It's going to be around indefinitely. And it has no peers among its wannabe competitors. It's a great opportunity. And you don't want to miss it. But, you will need to play by the rules, eBay's rules. If you don't, the feedback system can make success impossible for you on eBay.

There are three things you will want to understand before giving eBay a try. First, you will want to do things the eBay way. Why? Because it sells well on eBay. Second, you will want to make sure that you don't get any negative feedback. Why? Because it will kill your reputation before you get your business off the ground. Third, you will want to think through what you can provide in the way of customer service. People who shop online expect—and get—good customer service.

eBay Ways

To begin, read the eBay Community Values (*http://pages.ebay.com/ help/confidence/community-values.html*). Excerpts from the eBay Community Values:

> We believe people are basically good.
>
> We believe everyone has something to contribute.
>
> We believe that an honest, open environment can bring out the best in people.
>
> We recognize and respect everyone as a unique individual.
>
> We encourage you to treat others the way that you want to be treated.

Not only read it, but believe it. If you can adopt the attitude embodied by Community Values, you will be several steps ahead of many of your competitors. On eBay, you will be expected to be courteous, considerate, friendly, fair, and honest. If you are short any of these attributes, you may be headed for disaster as you try to sell vehicles on eBay.

Also read the eBay User Agreement (*http://pages.ebay.com/help/policies/user-agreement.html*).

If you look upon eBay as an opportunity to sell specific vehicles, you will do well. Many things that dealers do offline are designed to funnel hot prospects off the street into their used car lots. That's not necessary on eBay. The buyers are self-selected. They want something specific, and they look for it on eBay. If they don't get it from you, they'll get it from a competitor. In other words, eBay is not necessarily an opportunity to funnel prospective buyers to vehicles they have not selected.

As this is being written, there are over 200 Cadillac DeVilles available for purchase on eBay. If someone wants a DeVille, they will find it. If you have one for sale and they're not interested in yours, you won't find it easy to funnel them to a different vehicle. Wish them well and send them on their way. Another hot prospect will come along specifically interested in DeVilles. The great thing about eBay is that you will find ready, willing, and able buyers for whatever you sell. With the right price and a good attitude, you have a great chance of making plenty of sales.

Feedback

Don't take our word for it. Study the feedback system. It works. And it works well. To do well on eBay, that is, to sell successfully on eBay, you have to build a good reputation. Make no mistake, if you develop a poor feedback record on eBay, the number of buyers who will deal with you will shrink considerably.

If you have a poor feedback record on eBay, perhaps someone will take a chance on buying a $25 item from you. But few buyers will take a chance on buying a big-ticket item, such as a vehicle, from you.

If You're a Dealership

Our advice is to develop a bomb-proof strategy for building a sterling reputation *before* you start to sell on eBay. You just can't afford to take chances.

This is further complicated for a dealership by the question, Who do you permit to do the selling? Do you designate one salesperson? Do you allow any salesperson so long as they are familiar with eBay? Do you allow any salesperson so long as they can use a computer?

Five years from now, consultants will be telling you how to structure your eBay sales business. In the meanwhile, you have to understand that eBay is a unique market that requires a knowledgeable approach. Don't treat it lightly. Use some commonsense. Institute some controls. Don't let your dealership's activities on eBay be a free for all. Always remember that your feedback record stays with you forever.

Big Time Consultants

The big accounting-consulting firms already advise mid-size and large corporate clients how to sell on eBay.

If You're a Salesperson

If you're a salesperson, you have nothing to sell. Your dealership does. Do you offer vehicles in the name of your dealership? Or, do you offer them in your own name? What will the dealership permit you to do?

We recommend that you offer vehicles on your own eBay account but in the name of your dealer. That way, you have control over the sales and you can take your eBay account and feedback with you to your next place of employment. If you don't have your own eBay account and you start working at another dealership (without an eBay account) and must open a new account, you will start with zero feedback. With zero feedback, you will not be able to get as many bids, and the bidding won't go as high.

You are still operating in the digital wild west. Almost anything goes. Now is the time to build your personal *modus operandi* (method of operating) on eBay. Within five years, perhaps less, dealerships will take over eBay selling and bureaucratize it. (It's happening already.) Then you won't have any options. You will have to do it the dealership way. However, if you've developed your own *modus operandi* that works well and you have a good feedback record, a dealership might let you operate independently on eBay to sell vehicles.

The key here is your feedback record. It's public. A dealership might even check it before hiring you as a salesperson. In the future, a dealership is certain to check it before allowing you to sell its vehicles via eBay on your own eBay account.

eBay Community

Do you have to participate in the eBay community to be successful on eBay? The answer is "No." The active eBay community is quite small in comparison to the huge numbers of people actively and successfully selling on eBay. Nonetheless, the people who do participate in the eBay community exercise influence over eBay policies. Consequently, you need to be aware of the eBay community and it agenda so as to anticipate the direction in which eBay may go with its operations.

Naturally, if you want to change something about how eBay operates, the eBay community gives you a means to potentially bring about change.

The eBay community is also a huge reservoir of knowledge. When you have problems, you can turn to the eBay community (via Discussion Boards) to find solutions. Many eBay members generously devote their time to helping others resolve both technical and business issues in regard to doing business on eBay. Specifically, there is an eBay Motors Discussion Board.

Customer Service

People have come to expect great customer service online in general and on eBay in particular. A significant part of the eBay way is providing good customer service. This is particularly true for big-ticket items such as vehicles. In addition, about 75 percent of eBay Motors transactions take place across state lines. In many cases, a buyer travels to a distant city to complete a purchase transaction. This opens even more opportunities for dealers to provide helpful customer service to buyers.

Conclusion

Get in the groove, the eBay groove. eBay is a unique marketplace. To do well in any marketplace, you need to understand the byways. eBay is no different. Get a feel for how eBay members use this huge marketplace, pay attention to the eBay culture, play by the eBay rules, and you'll sell well on eBay.

19

Auction Management Services

Put three or four things up for sale on eBay, and suddenly you start to get the feeling that things might get out of control. It's just difficult to keep track of more than a few items without some sort of system. You can create a paper system yourself to keep track of the vehicles you auction on eBay, but a digital system is easier to use and more efficient.

Regardless of what you do, the penalty for not keeping track of your items will sooner or later be negative feedback. You must keep track. So, this chapter provides information on auction management services, which make it easy for you to keep track of several vehicles, several dozen vehicles, or several hundred vehicles. Indeed, many auction management services provide you with a wide range of services from inventory control to emailing auction follow-up.

Considerations

There are several choices you need to make before you take advantage of programming to conduct your eBay automotive business.

Program or Service?

Do you want a normal program (desktop program) that runs on your computer or a program delivered via the Web (i.e., a programming service) that runs in your Web browser? If you have wide bandwidth, the service has lots of advantages. If you use a dial-up connection to the Internet, a service might still work for you, but you have to be online to use it.

We recommend an auction management service such as the Andale software service delivered via the Web (*http://andale.com*). Here are some advantages:

- Can be used on any computer connected to the Internet.

- All programming is used through a Web browser.

- No maintenance required. Continually updated by vendor.

- Files saved online, presumably on a system that's backed up everyday.

- Reasonable monthly cost.

Of course, there's nothing wrong with normal (desktop) programming that you install on your computer and use like any other programs. If you're comfortable installing updates and learning a new interface, this kind of programming may be your best bet.

The truth is that the auction management services do provide some desktop programming that you install on your computer. On the other hand, most desktop auction management programs (installed on your computer) do have a Web component to them too. So, it's a mixed bag no matter which way you go, desktop or service. However, our experience dictates that a service ultimately saves you a lot of trouble. All you need is a computer, an operating system, a Web browser, and a connection to the Internet, and you can do your work anywhere, even on someone else's computer.

Scope of Services

Some software offerings are larger than others. You want to make sure that the desktop program or service you choose provides all the features you need. For instance, you will certainly need inventory control capability. If you already have such capability, however, you don't necessarily need to replicate it in your auction management service or software. Some providers even offer you a smorgasbord of services priced individually. You pick and choose and pay accordingly.

Learning Curve

Let's face it. When we talk about auction management services, we're talking accounting and account management software. These are not the easiest programs to learn. Most of us will struggle with software designed for programmers. But we thrive with software designed for novices. You will want to make sure that the programs you choose are easy for you to learn and use.

Cost

Costs vary widely. Enterprise systems (i.e., for corporate use) tend to be quite expensive. Auction management software for small businesses and simple businesses is surprisingly inexpensive. Unless you are a very large dealership, stick with the easy-to-use and inexpensive programs.

Integration

That brings us to integration. You can integrate auction management capabilities into your existing digital system. That requires custom programming and can be expensive. The best approach is to put your business on an auction management service first. Then from experience, decide which software features you need. At that point you can proceed more intelligently with your integration. Or, perhaps you will find that integration isn't cost-effective and will continue to use an auction management service.

Sample Service

For an example, let's look at Andale (*http://www.andale.com*), a veteran auction management service that offers a wide scope of services.

Andale

You can buy Andale services individually or in groups. The services offered include:

- Hot product advisory
- Price research
- Counters
- Professional counters
- Sales analyzer
- Sources of inventory
- Image posting
- Listing management
- Cross-selling system
- Storefront
- Customer checkout

- Email manager

- Feedback manager

- Refund management

- Listing ad creation

This is an impressive selection of services for general retail selling on eBay.

But Look at This

OK, the Andale offering looks inviting. But guess what? Andale has a specialty service for auto dealers called Andale Autos (*http://autos.andale.com*). Now we're talking. An auction management service just for vehicles!

Features

Here are the features of this special version of Andale tailored to vehicles, similar to the general Andale:

- Price research

- Counters

- Image posting

- Showroom

- Listing management

- Cross-selling system

- Refund management

If you're a dealer, you will want to study these services carefully.

Pricing

Although the general Andale services are priced individually, the Andale Autos services are offered as a package at one price.

Database Primer

In order to understand the possibilities of expanding your sales beyond eBay on the Web, we have to explore the use of databases. Databases fuel commerce. There are embedded databases in most business programs even though they may not be visible. The auction management services and programs are no different. They, too, use embedded databases to work their magic.

For a wide range of services you need a database table that holds a variety of information. That means multiple pieces of information. Let's say to provide inventory control services for an item you need 7 pieces of information. For example, you need the name of the product. A second piece of information you need might be the model number. To place an auction ad for an item, let's say you need 9 pieces of information. To create a store item ad for your eBay Store (see Chapter 20), let's say you need 6 pieces of information. Does that mean you need 22 (7 + 9 + 6) pieces of information in a database table? Not necessarily. Some of the pieces of information for each use will be the same. In other words, the information will overlap.

Let's say that you need only 15 pieces of information in a database table to provide the required data for inventory control, an auction ad, and an eBay Store ad. In digital language that means you need 15 fields (old terminology) or 15 columns (newer terminology) in the table. How do you get out the data you need for a particular purpose? You make a query to the database (table).

A query is simply a request for a certain set of data. Let's number the pieces of data 1 through 15. For inventory control you need data pieces 2,4,5,7,8,9,14 (total of 7 columns). The program queries the database and pulls out that specific data to use for inventory control. Next you need the pieces of data 1,2,3,5,8,10,11,13,15 (total of 9 columns) for an eBay auction ad. The program queries the database and pulls out that specific data to use for an eBay Auction ad. Finally, you need the pieces of data 4,6,9,11,12,15 (total of 6 columns) for an eBay Store ad. The program queries the database and pulls out that specific data to use for an eBay Store. Thus, from one compact table of data you can query and pull out three different sets of data, each for a specific purpose.

Inventory Control Query

    1
    2 —>
    3
    4 —>
    5 —>
    6
    7 —>
    8 —>
    9 —>
    10
    11
    12
    13
    14 —>
    15

eBay Auction Ad Query

    1 —>
    2 —>
    3 —>
    4
    5 —>
    6
    7
    8 —>
    9
    10 —>
    11 —>

```
12
13 —>
14
15 —>
```

eBay Store Query

```
1
2
3
4 —>
5
6 —>
7
8
9 —>
10
11 —>
12 —>
13
14
15 —>
```

And there you have it. From one database you can query and pull out multiple sets of data for multiple purposes.

Now, let's say that you're using an auction management service for your inventory control, your eBay auctions, and your eBay Store merchandise. What happens when you need to do something new or different? (to be continued in the next section)

Froogle et al

Google, the Web's most popular search engine by a wide margin, has invented Froogle. Froogle is just like Google except that it displays only commercial data. That is, it lists and displays only catalog-like listings of merchandise. Each listing is a product for sale. Where does Froogle find an almost unlimited number of listings of products? It enables sellers (vendors, retailers, dealers) to submit a data feed to Froogle in a specified format. You submit the data feed correctly and properly, and you suddenly have items on Froogle. Indeed, Google may be an even bigger marketplace than eBay for general shopping; and if it isn't yet, Froogle may help it get there in the future.

As this book went to press Froogle was still in beta (trial), and Google was not charging sellers to submit their data feeds to Froogle. Perhaps in the future when Froogle is mature and out of beta, it will start charging sellers. It may not be free forever.

The Database Angle

What is a data feed? It's simply what we've already discussed. It's a query to a database to pull out a specific set of data for a specific use. Let's say for the Froogle data feed we need the pieces of data 3,5,8,10,13 (total of 5 columns) out of our database of 15 columns. The auction management service queries the embedded database and pulls out that specific data to use for Froogle product ads.

Thus, databases look like magic. Just by a simple query, you can sell in a completely different marketplace in addition to eBay with almost no additional effort. Let's repeat that. *Just by a simple query, you can sell in a completely different marketplace in addition to eBay with almost no additional effort.*

The Marketplace Angle

Selling in a huge new marketplace simply by one mouse click (or several clicks) in an online program? It doesn't get any better than this. It is magic! Indeed, you can not only sell in another major marketplace quite easily with an auction management service (that supplies a Froogle data feed), but you have everything you need to run your

Froogle business too (e.g., inventory control). Consider this a big Wow!

Yahoo Shopping

Not to be outdone by Google and trailing Google miserably in search engine popularity, Yahoo has rushed its own new marketplace to the Web and is now open for business. And what do you need to sell merchandise in this new marketplace? You guessed it. A data feed. You need another query for your auction management service to provide the Yahoo Shopping data feed called by Yahoo its "product feed." And voila! You can sell in another substantial marketplace with little additional effort.

Boy, were we wrong when we said in the last subsection, "It doesn't get any better than this," in reference to Froogle. It's better to do both Froogle and Yahoo too.

The Two-System Marketplace

In *eBay the Smart Way* Third Edition published a few months before this book, Joe asked,

> Does Yahoo constitute a third major marketplace? Google has over 50 percent of the search engine market. Yahoo has only 20 percent. Will Google gain more market share at Yahoo's expense? Or, visa versa? Another question is, Does Amazon.com constitute a third major marketplace? It currently seems more like an online department store than a diversified marketplace. Will Amazon be able to maintain or increase its market share? Stay tuned folks. This contest is getting interesting.

> Right now, I'm calling it a *Two-System Marketplace* (eBay + Froogle). Or, perhaps a more accurate description will be eBay + search engine catalogs (i.e., Froogle and Yahoo). We'll soon see how this works out.

In the meantime, if you're an eBay seller, take a serious look at Froogle and Yahoo Product Search to see what they can do for you.

Need we say more than is quoted above? Better review the information available at the Froogle website (*http://froogle.com*) and the Yahoo Shopping website (*http://shopping.yahoo.com*) to determine how you can sell in these new marketplaces.

Note that Yahoo "Product Search" switched its name to Yahoo "Shopping" after it emerged from beta in September 2003. It then started charging substantial fees for clicks on product links, which may knock it out of competition with eBay and Froogle.

At the time this book went to press, Froogle was still in beta and free even though it commenced operation well before Yahoo Product Search. Froogle may charge fees after emerging from beta, and it will be interesting to see whether such fees will be as high as Yahoo's fees. If Froogle's fees are as high, such fees may knock it, too, out of competition with eBay.

Nitty Gritty

Now let's get down to the nitty gritty. To take advantage of these new online marketplaces, you need programming that provides the requisite data feeds. You need a Froogle data feed. You need a Yahoo Shopping "product" feed. And by the time you read this, there may even be other significant new marketplaces that you can reach with yet additional data feeds. Without the capability of generating additional data feeds conveniently, you will not be able to as easily sell in these new marketplaces. It's all a matter of programming. Make sure you use an auction management service that supplies this additional capability.

Be sure to take a look at Vendio (*http://www.vendio.com*), an eBay auction management service, formerly called Auction Watch, to review its Froogle data feed feature.

What Can You Sell?

What can you sell? We're not going to tell you that. Froogle has its guidelines, which you can get on the Froogle website. Since Froogle is changing and the products that it allows are changing, we will leave it to you to research what is allowed at the time you read this. Likewise, Yahoo has its changing guidelines.

The fact is that Froogle and Yahoo may not offer much to sellers of vehicles, motorcycles, RVs, boats, and the like yet. If your product (e.g., trucks) isn't included in the products allowed when you check, don't give up. Check back at a later date. Froogle and Yahoo will expand their categories over the next few years.

If Froogle and Yahoo Shopping don't have much to offer the readers of this book, why include this database discussion? Because there's no telling where a data feed might get you in the future. Databases are the past, present, and future of ecommerce, and you want to get ready with your data-based programming to take advantage of well-populated new marketplaces in which you can sell cost-effectively.

Data Feed Party

So, who needs Froogle or Yahoo Shopping? Let's have a data feed party. Let's see how many places we can send our data feed and get our vehicles or "Motors" products out there for sale. The party starts here but doesn't end here. This will be an ongoing inquiry for you: "Where can I send my data feed to get into another marketplace?" Or, better yet, "Where can I send my data feed to get into another marketplace *free?*"

Hey, eBay is a huge marketplace, and that's what this book is about. But the authors don't work for eBay and don't own stock in eBay. So, we can tell it like it is. And it's a fact that there are other large online marketplaces for "Motors" where you can place your vehicles. Go find them.

To give you a head start, we list below a number of places you can send your data feed (not necessarily all free):

AutoBase, *http://autobase.com*

AutoByTel, *http://autobytel.com*

AutoNetUSA, *http://autonetusa.com*

AutoTrader, *http://www.autotrader.com*

Autoweb, *http://autoweb.com*

CarSoup, *http://www.carsoup.com*

Cars.com, *http://www.cars.com*

CarSmart, *http://carsmart.com*

CarSpot, *http://carspot.com*

DiamondLot, *http://diamondlot.com*

Stoneage, *http://stoneage.com*

Incidentally, DiamondLot (both a service and a marketplace) advertises that it will provide "automated uploads" (data feeds) to all of the above marketplaces. Moreover, it also advertises that it can provide a data feed to almost any marketplace on the Web. Now, there's a service you will want to consider.

Get the details about listing products (e.g., vehicles) via a data feed from each individual website that sells vehicles. Then ask your auction management service to incorporate each data feed into their service. Or, use DiamondLot as your sales management service.; it's providing unlimited data feeds already.

Data Feed Party

In case you didn't catch the explanation, the term *data feed party* does not refer to a party with vodka on the rocks, Sushi snacks, and square dancing music. It refers to the process of sitting down and researching how many places you can send data feeds to sell in new marketplaces. So, have yourself a data feed party and see how many new marketplaces you can find to sell your vehicles or "Motors" merchandise with little additional effort.

Not the Best Idea

Just in case you haven't figured this out already, it's not the best idea to auction a vehicle (or whatever) on eBay and also sell it elsewhere at the same time. You may end up canceling too many auctions, which is not a good practice and is not going to make you popular on eBay. See Chapter 8. Consequently, the data feed party works best when a vehicle is offered continually at a fixed price (e.g., eBay Store – see Chapter 20), but not at auction.

Summary

Whether you choose auction management desktop software or an auction management service (software delivered via the Web), use something to keep your sales effort under control. If things get out of control, negative feedback is inevitable. Choose software or a service that gives you the capability to generate data feeds to get you into new marketplaces with little effort. eBay is a huge marketplace for vehicles, but it's not the only large marketplace in which you can sell.

20

eBay Store

Once upon a time, it was cool and sometimes even profitable to have an ecommerce website. But it has turned out that marketing on the Web is just as expensive as marketing off the Web, and getting your website found on the Web by potential customers requires a substantial marketing effort. Is there a better way?

As we discussed in Chapter 19, Froogle, Yahoo Shopping, and specialized automotive marketplaces may provide significant opportunities for you to sell without a website. Indeed, the idea of creating a catalog of your products somewhere just by providing a data feed is a powerful idea, and you certainly have many opportunities to put such an idea into effect, such as a data feed to AutoTrader.

But is there a way to have your cake and eat it too, that is, have a website without the burden of promoting it? There is. It's simple. Establish an eBay Store (cake) and build a robust *About Me* page (icing).

Let eBay Do the Talking

What does this crazy heading mean? It means let eBay do the promoting. eBay's name is a great attraction. eBay spends heavily on promotion and advertising. And eBay will give you a website in its online mall (for lack of a better word). In other words, let eBay deliver customers to you in your online storefront just as it delivers them to your online auctions.

Let's face it. eBay is a fabulous brand. It draws buyers (customers). But eBay doesn't sell anything (except eBay T-shirts). It simply provides an auction marketplace, which you can use for a reasonable fee. We might add, that the auction character of the marketplace is almost irrelevant. It's just a marketplace mechanism for sealing a deal. Indeed, about 50 percent of eBay sales are now fixed price (Buy It Now) making the auction character of eBay even less important.

But the auctions are oriented to *merchandise*. eBay is now lending its fabulous brand to *merchant-oriented* selling. eBay Stores are relatively new. They comprise, in effect, and online mall. Or, another way to view them is that they constitute a multi-vendor catalog. Whichever way you look at it, they provide you an opportunity to have a significant presence on the Web for a reasonable price. The eBay name is golden, and now you can be part of it with your own business (your own brand).

eBay Store

An eBay Store isn't necessarily pretty. eBay Stores are still a work in progress, and we must assume they will offer you more visual design flexibility in the future. What an eBay Store gives you is a permanent Web address (URL) where you can offer catalog items today and perhaps other attractions someday in the future. Your catalog items must be fixed price, and eBay Stores are not well integrated with eBay auctions.

Marketing

Are eBay Stores a complete Web marketing solution? The answer is clearly "No." eBay Stores are not well known or well used yet. Their primary use comes via links from eBay auctions. Every person auctioning who has an eBay Store has a red tag by their name. This alerts potential buyers that there may be additional similar merchandise at the seller's Store.

A Better Way

The red tag doesn't work very well. You need to be proactive to market your Store effectively. How do you do that?

In the good old days, eBay allowed a link from an auction ad to your independent website. In other words, you could use an auction ad to promote your website. That made having an independent website worthwhile. You could generate traffic to your website just by running auctions on eBay.

But eBay disallowed the link after it developed eBay Stores. That effectively devalued independent websites. You can still link to your website from your eBay *About Me* page, but it's not nearly as effective.

To effectively promote your eBay Store, you need to link to it from within your eBay Motors auction ads. Such links are allowed. The red tag in the auction head just isn't enough. In fact, you might even consider using multiple links to your Store inside an auction ad.

Remember also that your eBay Store has its own URL. There is nothing to prevent you from promoting your eBay Store as if it were an independent website. And having an eBay Store is less expensive than operating your own website.

A Specific Way

There's a specific way to promote your Store that works better than anything else. Systematically run auctions that include links to your Store in the body of the auction ads. You will get plenty of high-quality traffic (people who are interested in your items) from your auctions. The links will carry many prospective buyers over to your Store. This is particularly true if you sell a narrow range of products (e.g., high-end cars). It's less true if you sell a wide range of products.

If you don't want to auction your items and would rather sell them strictly at fixed prices, use the auctions anyway just to promote your Store. You can use the *Buy It Now* feature to fix the price in an auction or set the reserve to bring you a minimum price.

Specialization

The previous subsection points out that specialization works best for eBay Stores. Auctions (inherently specialized) will promote specialized Stores. Auctions don't necessarily promote unspecialized Stores.

For instance, suppose you specialize in selling high-end cars. Someone who looks at a Cadillac DeVille in your auction ad is likely to be interested, too, in the Lincoln Continental, Acura RL, and Lexus GS 300 that you have in your Store. If you don't specialize, however, the person who looks at the Cadillac DeVille in your auction ad is not likely to be interested in the Chevrolet Lumina, Mercury Mystique, Dodge Caravan, and Honda Civic you have in your Store.

In the Future

Some day eBay will learn to better integrate eBay Stores into eBay, and Stores will develop more traffic. No mall has ever been wildly successful on the Web, and eBay Stores are currently no exception. But eBay's name and the association of eBay Stores with eBay auctions provide a formula for potential success. This is one Web mall that has a good chance of becoming dominant eventually. In the meanwhile, a Store makes an inexpensive and effective substitute for an independent website.

A Website

An eBay Store is a website. You can use it as a your website. Someday you may even be able to put unlimited content (non-sales information) on it. You can use your Store's URL in your stationery, cards, and promotional literature. You can refer potential customers to it over the phone and by email. It's a real website, albeit with limitations.

Use a Forward

Suppose your have the URL *SuperMotors.com* but you don't want to operate an independent website. What can you do? Use a forward from *SuperMotors.com* to your eBay Store URL. It's just like having your own independent website hosted by eBay. Anyone using the URL *SuperMotors.com* will go straight to your eBay Store.

You can add artistic design to your Store, although the possibilities are limited. Try Elance (click on Professional Services on the eBay homepage) to find a skilled webworker who will make you an attractive eBay storefront for a reasonable price. Have them do a nice *About Me Page* for you, too, where you can promote your business in general.

Look for special features that will enable you to make your Store more useful. For example, eBay enables you to have your own custom search categories for searching through your Store. Categories might be sedans, coupes, vans, and SUVs. Or, they might be brand names. There will be similar enhancements in the future.

Merchandising Manager

The merchandising manager enables you to put a mini catalog of your items at the bottom of each of your auction ads and Store ads. It's a great cross-selling tool and should work well for vehicles, especially for dealerships that specialize in a certain line of vehicles.

Fees

Stores are evolving as are the fees for placing items in your Store. Check out the latest fee structure on the eBay website. The posting of items can be much longer than for eBay auctions.

About Me

The *About Me* webpage on eBay is your big opportunity to promote your business and do even more. You're only allowed one webpage, but you can put an unlimited amount of information on one webpage. Take advantage of it.

You will want to put a link to your *About Me* webpage in all your auction ads. You will also want to put a link to your *About Me* webpage in all your Store ads. Don't underestimate the power of telling people your story.

> SuperMotors was founded in 1983 by Dale G. Anderson, a retired IBM executive, and two employees. Today his sons Hank and Jim operate the business with 27 employees. Originally a Honda dealership, SuperMotors today has Honda, Isuzu, and Chrysler, franchises and is the third largest automobile dealer in the metro area. It is well known for its sponsorship of the local Wildcats soccer team, which has played in tournaments in 17 states...

The above is just a very small sample of what you can do. Actually, you can use HTML in your *About Me* webpage. That means you can incorporate images (e.g., photographs) and even other media. And you can link to an independent website if you have one.

Suppose you want to put educational material in your *About Me* webpage. Can you do that? Sure. For instance, suppose you want to provide a safety tutorial for driving a vehicle in the snow. You can do something reasonable and even lengthy in one webpage.

Suppose, however, you want to provide a series of tutorials on safe driving. Can you do that in one webpage? Theoretically, "Yes." As a practical matter, though, you might find yourself with a webpage that approaches infinity in length. eBay might tap you on the shoulder and say enough is enough. You would do better to break it up into multiple webpages. Unfortunately, eBay gives you only one webpage for *About Me*. But there's a way.

What Is a Website?

A website is a collection of linked webpages on a Web server—a host Internet service provider's (ISP's) hard disk—although theoretically it could be just one webpage. Usually, there's a home page (a beginning webpage) that links to the other webpages on the website. But does it have to be that way? Not necessarily. You can use webpages on different Web servers to cobble together a website; let's call it an *overall* website. Let's look at the case regarding the series of safety tutorials.

Putting Together a Overall Website

You want to use an independent website to supplement your *About Me* webpage (i.e., a place where you can publish vehicle safety tutorials). You also want to put together an overall website that promotes your business. The first consideration is, Does it make sense to do this? More specifically, if you are going to build a overall website using *About Me* as a home page, does it make sense to so without an eBay

Store? The answer is, "Sure." So long as you constantly run vehicle auctions, your overall website makes sense. If there are lapses where you have no auctions on eBay, however, your overall website is unlikely to get any traffic.

If you operate an eBay Store, your independent website supplements your Store effort. You always have inventory for sale in your eBay Store, and your independent website, where the tutorials are located, will get constant traffic. In other words, your overall website will have more visibility on the Web with constantly available inventory on eBay than without. Thus, running eBay vehicle auctions, operating an eBay Store, publishing a hearty *About Me* webpage, and running a supplementary independent website—all of which together constitute an overall website—make a viable ecommerce combination.

Three URLs

For your overall website, you will use three URLs.

The first will be your eBay Store. This is a unique and permanent Web address.

The second will be your eBay *About Me* webpage. This, too, is a unique and permanent Web address.

And the third will be at an independent URL; let's call it *supermotors.com*, named after the name of your business: SuperMotors.

eBay URLs

Your eBay URLs will look something like this:

Store

http://www.stores.ebay.com/id=1647510&ssPageName=L9

About Me

http://members.ebay.com/ebaymotors/aboutme/supermotors

Not simple but nonetheless functional.

Host ISP

A host ISP is a service that provides you with a website either with the ISP's domain name or your own domain name. Suppose the host ISP is FastServer with the domain name *fastserver.com*. Without your own domain name, your website URL might look like this:

http://www.fastserver.com/supermotors

Or, it could look like this:

http://supermotors.fastserver.com

Suppose you get the domain name *supermotors.com* and ask your host ISP to use it for your website. Your URL will be:

http://www.supermotors.com

Or, it could be:

http://supermotors.com

Or, it could be both. Now you have a URL for your independent website, a unique and permanent Web address.

Where's the Website?

The overall website spans three URLs. Here's how it might work:

Use your *About Me* webpage as your home page. Remember, eBay permits you to link to your own independent website from your *About Me* webpage. You can also link to your eBay Store.

Home Page

You can make your eBay *About Me* page into a robust home page for your overall website. It is a webpage, and you can use HTML in the page to do what any webpage can do.

Catalog (eBay Store)

Your eBay Store become the catalog of inventory on your overall website. You don't need any special catalog programming. Your Store is integrated into eBay and gets traffic via eBay. The ads for the item listings also link back to your home page (*About Me* webpage).

Content

Your independent website is where you can publish anything you want and thereby integrate it into your eBay presence. In this case, you want to present a series of driving safety tutorials via the Web to promote your vehicle sales. You can do so using as many webpages and as much Web media as you desire.

Auctions

In addition, you can link to your auctions from any webpage and visa versa (except that you can't link to your independent website from your auctions). This opens up a lot of possibilities. Unfortunately, auctions are ephemeral. They come and go. If you integrate them into your website, you will stay busy changing your website pages to update the links as the auctions are posted and then completed.

The Store Does It

Your eBay Store features your auction items and includes them and deletes them automatically as they come and go.

Put It All Together

Link it all together and you have an overall website that works well. But what about buyers? Aren't they going to be confused by all the changes in URLs? Certainly not. Even though the URL of the current webpage appears in the URL window in a browser, no one pays attention to it. Your 3-URL overall website can be as seamless as any website at one URL. Remember, you control the links that you put in the pages at all three URLs.

Conclusion

Creating an overall website makes more sense than establishing a separate self-autonomous website—but an independent supplementary website can be included in the overall website. This makes the most sense when used with an eBay Store. The Store provides a catalog and constant inventory. You can use you About Me page to be the home page for your overall website.

Exceptions

There are two exceptions to the idea set forth in this section. First, if you're already running an independent website and it's successful, keep it going. We're not here to argue with success. Second, the idea for this section is not rigid. It is likely that you have special needs for your particular online sales efforts. Adapt this idea to your needs and come up with a hybrid scheme that works for you. The primary point that we're trying to make in this chapter is that eBay Stores and the About Me page provide you with significant opportunities to expand your online sales cost-effectively.

Recommendation

If you want to sell your entire inventory on eBay—or at least keep constant inventory on eBay—then an eBay Store makes a lot of sense and will help you sell more. If you want to have a website to promote your business, a separate self-autonomous website may not be your best way to promote. It takes a lot of marketing to build traffic at a separate website. A better and more cost-effective way may be to build a 3-URL overall website, which incorporates your inventory as well as your content.

Look to the auction management services to assist you in the goals for your business. The hands-on discussion of URLs above was not necessarily intended to provide you with hands-on skills. It was provided to show you the possibilities. The auction management services can handle the details for you. If they can't, then turn to the specialized vehicle auction management services to help meet your goals and promote your business on the Web.

Keep in mind that the key to greater sales outside eBay auctions is the eBay Store. It's your opportunity to establish something comparable to a separate website or, better yet, to integrate the Store into an overall website with great possibilities.

Finally, remember from Chapter 19, that an eBay Store is just another data feed.

VI

Other Sales

21

Parts & Accessories

eBay Motors is just the right place to auction automotive parts and accessories. In fact, we have purchased parts just after buying used vehicles on eBay. When you buy a used vehicle, there's often some little thing you need, and those little things tend to be expensive when you buy them from dealers. It's cheaper to buy them on eBay if you can find them.

Someday it comes time to sell. Before you put the vehicle up for auction on eBay, you need to get it in as good as shape as possible. And you often need parts. Again, we have found such parts on eBay.

But you don't have to be buying or selling a vehicle on eBay to seek parts on eBay. Just owning any vehicle is trouble enough. And mechanics charge $50 to $90 per hour for labor. If it's a part that you need now, you might be able to find it on eBay and install it yourself.

Each vehicle has thousands of parts, and eBay doesn't even come close to covering all the parts, even for one model of one vehicle for one year. Nevertheless, there are always hundreds of thousands of parts and accessories available on eBay. It's a good fishing grounds. You might just find what you need. If you do, it's normally convenient and inexpensive to buy it on eBay. And if it's not there today, it may be there next week or next month.

Parts for Us All

Buying parts is not limited to mechanics. We can all use vehicle parts on certain occasions.

Recent Example

Joe needed to sell his 1989 Cadillac in early 2004 after buying a Lincoln Town Car. The front left turn signal lens was broken (vandalism). It detracted from the appearance of an otherwise beautiful car. So, Joe searched for a replacement on eBay. Here's what he found:

1. Under Lighting & Lamps, 56,587 items.

2. Under Lighting & Lamps, Cadillac, 410 items.

3. 1989-93 Cadillac De Ville front left turn signals, 4 items.

With another search he found:

1. Under Lighting & Lamps, 56,587 items.

2. Under Lighting & Lamps, Turn Signals, 3,062 items.

3. Under Lighting & Lamps, Turn Signals, Cadillac, 6 items.

4. 1989-93 Cadillac De Ville front left turn signals, 1 item.

Anyone can replace a broken turn signal lens. Even Joe. It's not difficult. For $20 in parts and a few minutes labor, the Cadillac looked like new.

Limitations

One practical limitation on auto parts commerce via eBay is delivery (transportation cost). Parts that are small and light sell well on eBay. The shipping isn't a deal killer. Parts that are large, heavy, and inexpensive will not sell well on eBay. The shipping is a deal killer. Consequently, eBay is not your best source for all the vehicles parts you may need.

Buying to Sell

Using eBay parts and accessories is a great way to get a used vehicle ready for sale without spending a lot of money. You don't need new parts. The vehicle isn't new. Used parts will do just fine. It might be worth your trouble to buy used parts even if it takes a mechanic to install them.

Parts Buyers Be Careful

When you buy parts, it's a good time to be precise. A vehicle has thousands of parts. There are hundreds of different vehicles. It's quite easy to make a mistake when trying to obtain parts. Be very careful and double check to make sure the part you buy on eBay is exactly what you need.

Parts Sellers Take Note

Buying parts is sometimes a difficult task for those who need them. The more information you can provide on each part, the easier time the buyer will have in making a buying decision. A reluctant buyer, who isn't sure, doesn't bid as much.

It's essential to provide photographs. Parts catalogs often have photographs or expensive-to-make drawings that enable a person to see just what they're getting. An illustration or photograph is an essential means of determining whether the part is the right one.

Parts for Real Mechanics

Professional mechanics usually need parts immediately and cannot buy parts on eBay and wait for them to arrive. But eBay is still another source of parts that comes in handy occasionally. A home mechanic who has a long-term project in the garage may find eBay a good source of parts.

Professional Mechanics

eBay Motors is a place to perhaps find a part that you can't find elsewhere (see Figure 21.1).

Figure 21.1   eBay Parts & Accessories subcategories. ©1995-2004 eBay Inc.

It may also be a place to find parts inexpensively for less affluent customers who can't afford to pay for an original manufacturer's parts. Under the *Parts & Accessories* category, there are dozens of subcategories.

For instance, in late 2003 eBay showed 7,416 items under *Transmission & Drivetrain*. The subcategory of *Automatic Transmission & Parts* showed 1,469 items. These tend to be heavy items, expensive to ship. Let's take a look at some lighter items. The *Air Intake & Fuel Delivery* category showed 14,514 items. The subcategory *Carburetors* showed 1,298 items.

Unfortunately, when you're serving customers daily, the eBay process may not be fast enough to get parts in a timely manner. But for long-term projects it can be another valuable source.

Home Mechanics

Thousands of people are trained mechanics but have another career. Yet many dabble in rebuilding vehicles at home or casually repair family or friends' vehicles.

Mr. Secretary Rebuilds

Colin Powell, US Secretary of State, is a prime example. Apparently his hobby is rebuilding Volvos in his garage. It would be interesting to know if he has ever used eBay Motors to get parts.

Such people don't normally need new parts, and they can often wait a few days or a few weeks for parts to arrive. eBay makes a great place to look for the parts they need.

Alternatives

What are the alternatives to buying on eBay? First, you can go to an auto parts store. There is a huge industry that manufactures common parts for vehicles at prices generally less expensive than the original equipment manufacturers (OEMs). However, as we all have experienced, the selection in auto parts stores is somewhat limited. Most such parts are for normal maintenance and replacements.

Second, you can go to a junkyard. There you can get OEM parts from vehicle wrecks. But there is no guarantee that a particular junkyard will have what you need. There are also junkyards that offer parts on the Internet.

Finally, you can go to an auto dealer and order parts from the original manufacturer. This is usually an expensive option.

Summary

Perhaps more so for home mechanics or for non-mechanics rather than professional mechanics, eBay is a rewarding source to find the parts you need. There are hundreds of thousands of parts appearing on eBay Motors. You no longer need to pay big bucks for some small plastic thing. If you can't find what you need today. Look next week.

22

Other Motors

Cars and pickup trucks are not the only vehicles sold on eBay Motors. This chapter covers motorcycles, power boats, ATVs (all terrain vehicles), RVs and campers, commercial trucks, and collector cars. These are all eBay categories with over 500 vehicles for sale each week. Other eBay Motors categories with less than 500 listings each week are not covered.

The guidelines are the same for selling almost any motorized vehicle. The resources change. Thus, in this chapter we provide resources for the categories named above. If your vehicle has been left out, what can you get from this book?

General Principles

Let's review the general principles of dealing in motorized vehicles so that you can relate what you've learned in this book to the motorized vehicle you want to buy or sell.

Price

As we said many times, even in other books, the greatest auction technique for buyers or sellers is to know the value. For cars and trucks, knowing the value is easy. Just get online and browse Edmunds.com. Not all vehicles, however, have published statistics on prices. You might need to find another way to determine values. Perhaps you can find current values in specialty magazines that have a price issue annually. Or, look for local advertising publications (usually free) to see the prices at which various similar vehicles are offered. Check the classified ads in newspapers. Check with dealers selling used vehicles.

Whatever you do, don't bypass eBay. You can always get pricing information from the completed auctions that eBay archives for about three weeks. Indeed, there's always pricing information available for those who are willing to dig for it.

Kelley

You can find pricing information for the following motor vehicles in the Kelley Blue Book online (*http://www.kbb.com*):

- Motorcycles
- ATVs
- Personal watercraft
- Snowmobiles

NADA

You can find pricing information for the following motor vehicles in the NADA guide online (*http://www.nada.com*):

- Classic cars
- Motorcycles
- Snowmobiles
- ATVs
- Personal watercraft
- Power boats
- Sailboats
- RVs
- Aircraft

Black Book

The Black Book (*http://www.blackbookusa.com*) provides prices for motorcycles and classic cars. This is a subscription service.

Quality

A quality check for cars and trucks is easy. You make a visual inspection, take a test drive, run a vehicle history, and have a mechanic check the vehicle. It doesn't take too much imagination to understand that this approach applies to all motorized vehicles with the possible exception of obtaining a vehicle history. Review Chapter 5 to remind yourself how to engineer quality checks into the deal.

Now, it's easy to overlook one of these important quality tests. But if you do, you may be ultimately disappointed. For instance, suppose you want to buy a 20-foot boat with a 75-horsepower outboard motor. It's on a trailer in the seller's garage, and the nearest lake is 20 miles away. Should you really insist on taking it for a test drive? You bet! Perhaps the seller won't be too thrilled taking you for a test drive on first contact. However, after you've negotiated the deal and all other contingencies are removed, insist that the seller take you on a test drive as the last contingency before finalizing the deal. Of course, there are sellers who will take you on a test drive as the first order of business. You know, any excuse to go boating.

What can you find out on a test drive? A lot more than you can find out in the garage. For instance, if the boat leaks, it should become obvious during the test drive. It may not be obvious in the garage.

Unfortunately, a vehicle history may not be available for other vehicles as it is for cars and trucks. But it doesn't hurt to ask. If you're going to buy the 20-foot boat and the seller says she isn't aware of any service that provides a public record history in her state, go ask a boat dealer as well. Perhaps there is something similar in that state.

Negotiating

Negotiating guidelines are the same for most buying and selling situations. Negotiating is not about the vehicle. It's about satisfying the needs and wants of the buyer and seller. The principles are the same regardless of the vehicle. Chapter 16 gives you some good tips.

Financing

Financing differs from category to category. What is normal for boats might be considered expensive for cars and trucks. But the one principle that remains the same is to negotiate financing separately from the price of the vehicle on terms you can understand. Once the financing gets mixed up in the deal, you're out of your element and at someone else's mercy. Always consider the financing separately.

Calculate your loan payment at:

http://automotivemileposts.com/ads/calculator.html

Insurance

You've got to have insurance for everything with a motor. Take a look at your homeowner's insurance to see what it might cover in addition to your home. Perhaps nothing motorized, but until you look or inquire, you won't know. Don't worry about getting hefty collision or theft insurance on inexpensive vehicles. Do worry about liability. Make sure you have liability insurance that covers all potential accidents. The three key words to using insurance wisely for vehicles are not necessarily collision, damage, and theft. They are liability, liability, and liability.

Warranties

Warranties are widely available for cars and trucks, even used cars and trucks. And that's it. You're probably not going to find warranties for other used vehicles. Sure, it doesn't hurt to inquire. But don't count on finding warranty protection except, perhaps, what is left of the manufacturer's warranty.

Shipping

The story of shipping is finding specialized shippers. For instance, if you take a boat down to your local truck terminal for shipping, the shipping anywhere will probably cost more than the boat. Nevertheless, there are specialty boat shippers that will ship your boat professionally and less expensively. Seek specialty shippers when you can't take the time or trouble to go to a distant city to bring the vehicle home.

Now, different vehicles have different delivery situations than cars and trucks. If you travel to a distant city where the car or truck is located to do your inspections and close the deal, you can drive the vehicle home. When you travel to a distant city to inspect and close the deal on a 20-foot boat, you can't drive it home unless your means of travel to the distant city is your car or truck; then you can tow it home. As a practical matter, you may have to fly to inspect the boat and close the deal and then fly home. In that case, you will have to have the boat shipped home.

Legalities

The legalities for cars, trucks, motorcycles, and RVs are very similar from one state to another. The transaction documentation is similar too. For other types of vehicles, however, titles and licenses may vary widely from state to state and from vehicle to vehicle. You want to make sure that you do the paperwork for your transaction properly so that you don't have any unexpected problems or liabilities. Local dealers can help inform you.

A good place to start looking is the department of motor vehicles (DMV) or whatever it's called in your state. Go to Online DMV (*http://www.onlinedmv.com/index.html*) to find your DMV.

Where's the Information

The bottom line is that you will have to do some research to learn the peculiarities of each type of vehicle and its market. Where can you get the information you need?

Magazines

The first place to look is in specialty magazines. Go to Borders, Barnes & Noble, or a local independent bookstore to the magazine rack and see what's available. Supermarkets or convenience stores are other good places to look for these magazines. If you're buying a 20-foot boat with an outboard motor, there are several boating magazines that will provide you with valuable information. Even some fishing magazines might point you in the right directions.

Not Just the Content

It's not just the content of magazines that provide you the information you need. It's the advertising too. How do you find out something about insurance for the 20-foot boat? Perhaps from a marine insurance company that advertises in a boating magazine.

Dealerships

Another good place to go is a dealership. Most dealers are well versed on their market and the vendors serving that market. Most will know where much of the information you need is located, if it exists. You don't have to go very far to find a boat dealer to learn about buying and owning a 20-foot boat.

Clubs

Clubs and organizations are good places to find people who know something. Hang out for a short time at a club or organization (e.g., attend a meeting); meet some people; and ask them a lot of questions. You may want to join the organization after you make your purchase, but in the meanwhile you can talk with club members to discover the sources of the information you need. For a 20-foot boat, you might find people who can help you in a fishing club, an outdoor club that includes boating, or a boating club. (Or, you might go and hang out at a marina.) Many clubs and organizations even have websites where they provide information to the general public.

Web Search Engines

Don't, of course, overlook the Web search engines such as Google to find the information you need. It's amazing what you can find on the Web and how quickly and easily you can find it.

eBay Motors

Check out eBay as well. eBay can be a good source for pricing information as mentioned earlier. But it also may prove to be a good place to find vendors serving a specific vehicle market. eBay may even assemble information valuable to buying and selling a particular type of vehicle and post it on eBay for everyone to use. Expect to find eBay doing more and more of that in the years ahead.

Andale Autos

Andale Autos, an auction management service for eBay Motors, provides a research service that can give you robust pricing information. It's a subscription service, but the first month is free.

Discussion Boards

Finally, check out appropriate communities on the Internet. Join online discussion groups, communities, forums or whatever else they might be called. You will certainly find one about the vehicle you want to buy or sell, and the participants can give you assistance (answer your questions). Then too, don't overlook eBay. It has a list of *Discussion Boards* that may include your vehicle such as "Motorcycle Boulevard." And oh yes, there is a Discussion Board about "eBay Motors" too.

General Information

Some general sources of information that are valuable for more than one type of vehicle are:

Trader Online, *http://www.traderonline.com*

Deals on Wheels, *http://www.dealsonwheels.com*

Andale Autos (research), *http://autos.andale.com/motors/corp/products/research.jsp*

This section is followed by specialized sections for each of the high volume motor vehicle categories on eBay Motors.

Motorcycles

Motorcycles are money-saving basic transportation for many. For others, they are recreational transportation. They are the closest category to autos. For instance, many companies that finance or insure autos will also finance or insure motorcycles.

Magazines

American Iron, http://www.americanironmagazine.com

Cycle World, http://www.cycleworld.com

Motor Cyclist, http://www.motorcyclist.com

Pricing

Black Book (guide book), *http://www.blackbookusa.com*

Deals on Wheels, http://www.dealsonwheels.com

Kelley Blue Book (guide book), *http://www.kbb.com*

NADA Guide, *http://www.nada.com*

Truck, Race, Cycle, and Rec Marketplace (magazine), *http://www.dealsonwheels.com*

Financing

Capital One Auto Finance, 800-689-1789, *http://www.capitaloneautofinance.com*

eBay Financing Center, *http://www.financing-center.com*

E-Loan, 888-533-5333, *https://www.eloan.com*

Insurance

Progressive Insurance, 888-438-0867, *http://www.progressive.com*

Foremost Insurance Group, 800-237-6136, *http://www.foremost.com*

Markel American Insurance, 800-236-2453, *http://www.bike-line.com*

Shipping

1aa Motorcycle Transport, 888-347-1391, *http://www.1aamotorcycles.com*

Eagle One Express, 209-483-8925, *http://www.eagleonexpress.com*

Enclosed Vehicle Transport, 888-827-6799, *http://www.enclosedvehicletransport.com*

Shipmy Vehicle, 877-512-2227, *http://www.shipmyvehicle.com*

Collector Cars

This is a broad category. It includes antique cars and trucks, high performance cars, and hot rods.

Magazines

Car Collector, http://www.carcollector.com

Pricing

Black Book (guide book), *http://www.blackbookusa.com*)

Deals on Wheels, http://www.dealsonwheels.com

Dupont Registry Automobiles (magazine)*, http://www.dupontregistry.com*

Hemmings Motor News (magazine)*, http://www.hemmings.com*

NADA Guide, *http://nada.com*

Truck, Race, Cycle, and Rec Marketplace (magazine), *http://www.dealsonwheels.com*

Financing

Classic Car Financial, 877-527-7228, *http://www.classiccarfinancial.com*

Credit Corp USA, 954-771-2440, *http://www.creditcorpusa.com*

J.J. Best Banc, 800-872-1965, *http://www.jjbest.com*

Capital One, 800-689-1789, *http://www.automotivemileposts.com/financingperson.html*

Insurance

Condon & Skelly, 800-257-9496, *http://www.condonskelly.com*

Hagerty, 800-762-2628, *http://www.hagerty.com*

J.C. Taylor Antique Auto Insurance Agency, 800-345-8290, *http://www.jctaylor.com*

American Hobbyist Insurance, 800-395-4835, *http://www.americanhobbyist.com*

Shipping

Blue Highways, 800-622-6601, *http://www.bluehighways.net*

Horseless Carriage Carriers, 800-631-7796, *http://www.horselesscarriage.com*

Passport Transport, 800-325-4267, *http://www.passporttransport.com*

Newman International, 813-221-5000, *http://www.newmaninternational.com*

Thomas C. Sunday, 717-697-0939, *http://www.sundayautotransport.com*

ATVs

People use all terain vehicles (ATVs) for outdoor work and hunting as well as for general recreation. These vehicles can be expensive purchased new. Better to buy them used on eBay Motors.

Magazines

All-Terrain Vehicle, http://www.atvmagazine.com

ATV Illustrated, http://www.atvillustrated.com

ATV Magazine, http://www.atvnews.com

ATV Rider, http://www.atvrideronline.com

Pricing

Deals on Wheels, *http://www.dealsonwheels.com*

Kelley Blue Book (guide book), *http://www.kbb.com*

NADA Guide, *http://www.nada.com*

Financing

Bombardier Capital, 518-758-6507, *http://www.xtremepower-sports.com/Financing/financing.html*

Capital One Auto Finance, 800-689-1789, *https://www.capitaloneauto-finance.com/Public/ApplyNow/Default.aspx*

Insurance

ATV Line, 888-755-4288, *http://www.atv-line.com*

Progressive, 888-438-0867, *http://www.progressive.com*

Shipping

Aardvark Auto Relocation, 888-866-4020, *http://www.aard-varkauto.com*

RVs & Campers

This is an industry that's expanding. With more and more RVs on the road, this category will continue to grow significantly.

Magazines

Camping Life, http:/www./campinglife.com

Highways (Good Sam Club), *http://www.goodsamclub.com*

Motor Home, http://www.motorhomemagazine.com (see Figure 22.1)

Trailer Life, http://www.trailerlife.com

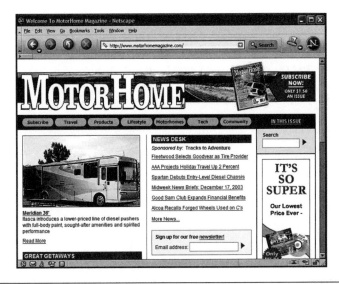

Figure 22.1   Motor Home website ©2003 Affinity Group Inc.

Pricing

Deals on Wheels (magazine), *http://www.dealsonwheels.com*

NADA Guide, *http://nada.com*

RV Search, *http://www.rvsearch.com*

Truck, Race, Cycle, and Rec Marketplace (magazine), *http://www.dealsonwheels.com*

Financing

Excel Credit, 407-862-2225, *http://www.excelcredit.com*

Good Sam RV Finance (Good Sam Club - Ganis Credit Corporation), 800-444-1476, *http://www.goodsamrvfinance.com*

New Coast Financial Services, 877-559-8937, *http://www.newcoastfinancial.com*

Financial Underwriters Network, 800-231-4003, *http://www.funloan.com*

RV Credit Direct, 888-656-9400, *http://www.beaconcredit.com*

Insurance

Gilbert RV Insurance, 888-784-6787, *http://www.rv-insurance.com*

Miller Insurance Agency, 800-622-6347, *http://www.millerrvinsurance.com*

Progressive Insurance, 888-539-7415, *http://www.progressive.com*

RV America Insurance, 800-400-0186, *http://www.rv-insurance-coverage.com*

VIP Insurance (Good Sam Club - GMAC Insurance), 800-847-2886, *http://www.goodsamvip.com*

Shipping

Allstates Worldwide, 800-338-8850, *http://www.aswd.com*

American RV Transfer, 909-704-6592, *http://www.browna.freeyellow.com*

Auto/Van/RV Delivery, 574-534-4250, *http://www.auto-van-rv-delivery.com*

Hoosier RV Transport, 574-848-7000, *http://www.hoosier-rv-transport.com*

RV Transport, 888-333-1664, *http://www.rvtransport.com*

Commercial Trucks

Anyone who wants to buy or sell a commercial truck will likely have knowledge in regard to their industry resources. We can't cover all the industries that use specialized commercial trucks. Instead, we have included a few resources primarily for the trucking industry, which includes many independent operators.

Magazines

Land Line, http://www.landlinemag.com

PayLoad, http://www.payloadmagazine.com

Pricing

Deals on Wheels, *http://www.dealsonwheels.com*

Truck Trader Online, *http://www.trucktraderonline.com*

Financing

DEPS, 866-406-3377, *http://driverandequipment.com*

Riviera Finance, 800-872-7484, *http://wwwriverafinance.com*

Insurance

1st Guard, 800-995-4827, *http://www.1stguard.com*

National Independent Truckers Insurance, 800-726-8376, *http://www.directtruckinsurance.com*

Western Truck Insurance Services, 800-937-8785, *http://www.truckinsure.com*

Shipping

AAA Discount Auto & Truck Transporters, 888-577-5400, *http://www.autoandtruckshippers.com*

Transportation Specialists, 626-968-4904, *http://www.transspecialists.com*

Power Boats

Power boats make up a significant eBay Motors category. The information below will help you get a good start on buying or selling a power boat.

Magazines

Motor Boating, http://www.motorboating.com

Boating, http://www.boatingmag.com

Yachting, http://www.yachtingnet.com

Pricing

Deals on Wheels, *http://www.dealsonwheels.com*

Dupont Registry Boats (magazine), *http://www.dupontregistry.com* (see Figure 22.1)

NADA Guide, *http://nada.com*

Financing

Beacon Marine Credit, 888-656-9400, *http://www.beaconcredit.com*

Excel Credit, 407-862-2225, *http://www.excelcredit.com*

Financial Underwriters Network, 800-231-4003, *http://www.funloan.com*

Intercoastal Financial Group, 800-916-0065, *http://www.boatloans.net*

New Coast Financial Services, 877-559-8937, *http://www.newcoastfinancial.com*

Sterling Associates, 888-286-7771, *http://www.boatbanker.net*

Figure 22.2   Dupont Registry website. ©2002 Dupont Registry.

Insurance

Total Dollar, 800-962 5659, *http://www.totaldollar.com*

Boat Insurance Store, 800-553-7661, *http://www.boatinsurancestore.com*

Hagerty, 800-762-2628, *http://www.hagerty.com*

Shipping

1stAboard, *http://www.1staboard.com*

ABM Transport, 321-303-4695, *http://www.abmtransport.com*

Associated Boat Transport, 800-247-1198, *http://www.associatedboat.com*

Captain Don W. Harper, 727-867-9466, *http://www.yachtdeliveries.com*

Hight Marine Transport, 800-519-2248, *http://www.boat-transportation.com*

Marine-Movers Boat Transport, 866-428-5262, *http://www.marine-movers.com*

Odege Yacht Delivery, 819-838-5265, *http://www.odegedelivery.com*

Zgram, 561-842-9368, *http://www.zgramyachtdeliveries.com*

23

Other Marketplaces

You can use eBay as a local auction. Go *Browse* (on the navigation bar), *Regions*. There you will find a list of nearly 70 metro areas. A subset of the normal eBay auctions is presented for each metro area. It's just like having a local auction for each city. Well, not exactly. The eBay local auctions have never been very exciting, although occasionally they are useful. The fact is that eBay hasn't figured out how to do local auctions well yet. But Craig Newmark has. Mr. Newmark has figured out how to create effective local marketplaces.

Craig's List

Try Craig's List (*http://www.craigslist.com*) for local marketplace action. It's not an auction, but that's irrelevant for this discusson. It's an exciting local marketplace. It started in the San Francisco Bay Area a long time ago—just like eBay—but over the years it has expanded to about 45 other cities. It is a mature marketplace in the Bay Area and some of the early additional cities (e.g., New York). It is just picking up steam in many other cities. It uses a different marketplace system than eBay, a system that seems to work effectively.

Craig's List doesn't have the security that eBay does, but then everything is local. Presumably, the threat of law enforcement is a realistic deterrent locally to those who might decide to break the law. Chances are that you will meet the other party when you purchase something from Craig's List. Indeed, it is more like a local classified ad marketplace than an online auction marketplace. You are permitted to place a specific ad only in one city, not in multiple cities.

What's the point? The point is that in the Bay Area and some of the early additional cities, Craig's List is a great place to buy and sell vehicles. As Craig's List matures in more cities, it will become a great place to buy and sell vehicles in those cities too. It's beyond the scope of this book to cover Craig's List in detail, but it's not a marketplace you will want to overlook when you buy or sell a vehicle.

Craig's List is easy to use—perhaps easier than eBay—and has less restrictions than most online marketplaces. This may explain it's popularity. It's a great place to sell older, less valuable vehicles that buyers will not travel out of state to pick up. And it's a great place to buy such vehicles as well.

Because its ads are so unstructured, Craig's List doesn't seem to be a candidate for a data feed. Nonetheless, databases are quite flexible these days, and a data feed can easily place an ad on Craig's List—if Mr. Newmark will accept the data feed.

That may not happen. Mr. Newmark's philosophy seems to be to keep the Craig's List vehicle For Sale section primarily for non-commercial use. Were a lot of local dealers to flood Craig's List with an abundance of over-priced used vehicles—as they do in most online vehicle marketplaces—Craig's List would lose its present character and perhaps much of its appeal. Thus, for individuals who want to sell their cars and trucks locally, especially older cars and trucks, Craig's List makes a great online marketplace to do so.

Perhaps more important right now is that Craig's List has reached a critical mass in the Bay Area and some other cities, such as New York. We assume it will reach a critical mass in many additional cities before long. Thus, it qualifies as a major marketplace nationally and a late-blooming competitor to eBay, *but only in local markets*.

So long as eBay continues to run its local auctions in a lackluster manner, there remains a huge void in the online auction industry. A huge opportunity! And Craig's List is filling that void, not with an auction, but with a fresh concept in online marketplaces.

If you're looking for a vehicle locally, give Craig's List a try. If you're an individual who wants to sell a vehicle locally, give Craig's List a try. If you're a dealer, Craigs List probably isn't for you; nonetheless, you can place vehicle listings individually on Craig's List.

If you're in a city where Craig's List is relatively new, you may not find many vehicles for sale. It's just a matter of time, however, before your version of Craig's Lists matures, and you will be able to find plenty of vehicles for sale.

Other Online Vehicle Marketplaces

Although we give dealers a detailed explanation in Chapter 19 on how to extend their sales to other online vehicle marketplaces, such as DiamondLot, we don't provide the same information for individual sellers. So, to end this eBay book on a seditious note, we provide below two major Web vehicle marketplaces, which we recommend, where individuals can buy and sell vehicles online successfully:

AutoTrader, *http://www.autotrader.com*

Cars.com, *http://www.cars.com*

Most major online vehicle marketplaces are strictly for dealer used vehicles. Buyers will find local dealer used vehicles there but not vehicles for sale by private parties. Private sellers are simply not permitted to list their vehicles in most major online vehicle marketplaces.

Even though AutoTrader and Cars.com list an excess of overpriced dealer used vehicles, much like their competitors, they also accommodate individual sellers. In doing so, they provide useful marketplaces for both individual buyers and sellers and give eBay Motors noticeable competition.

How To

How do you use these three online marketplaces that provide competition to eBay Motors? It's easy. Just go to Craig's List, AutoTrader, or Cars.com and follow the instructions at the websites. Keep in mind that most of what you learn in this book is just as applicable to buying and selling on these three websites as it is on eBayMotors. Consequently, even if you make all your used vehicle deals on these websites, the information, principles, and guidelines that this book provides will help you.

Good luck!

Appendix I Top 10 Tips for Buyers

The top 10 tips for success on eBay Motors for buyers follow below, not necessarily in order of priority:

Learn the Used Vehicle Game. Read this book or another book that sheds light on how vehicle dealers operate. Knowing the game will help you when buying from a private party and is absolutely necessary when buying from a dealer.

Tap the National Market. eBay Motors provides you with more choices and more opportunities to get the vehicle you want.

Research Market Value. Your best buying technique is to know the value of the vehicle you want to buy. With an accurate value, you can make smart decisions.

Use Quality Checks. Inspections and reports can help ensure that you will get a vehicle that runs well.

Buy with a Contingency Agreement. Buy only from a seller who will make the purchase contingent on your and your mechanic's inspections of the vehicle.

Analyze the Financing. Make sure you don't get taken to the cleaners with dealer financing. Always negotiate the purchase and the financing separately.

Get a Warranty. You can buy a warranty for a used vehicle. If you buy wisely, it's cost-effective vehicle protection and a good investment.

Protect Yourself. Don't be paranoid, but don't be careless either. Follow protective practices that make sense.

Pay Attention to Detail. Vehicle transactions are complex. Stay alert even when a dealer or a bank is handling the details of the transaction.

Keep a Cheerful Attitude. Negotiating and buying a vehicle is a serious business. But it can be fun too. Being pleasant can go a long way toward solving difficult problems when the going gets rough.

This top 10 list does not guarantee success for every vehicle purchase, but it will help you start to develop an intelligent and cost-conscious approach to buying on eBay Motors.

Appendix II Top 8 Tips for Sellers

The top 8 tips for success on eBay for sellers follow below, not necessarily in order of priority:

Take Advantage of the National Market. eBay Motors provides you with hundreds of potential buyers waiting to buy a vehicle like yours.

Research Market Value. Your best selling technique is to know the value of your vehicle. With an accurate value, you can more easily and more quickly make a sale.

Put Yourself in the Shoes of the Buyer. You're asking a lot of a buyer in another city to buy your vehicle. Make it easy for her.

Don't Hold Back. When you write your auction ad, give ample and complete information on the vehicle. eBay puts no limitation on the amount of text.

Show Many Photographs. Post at least a half-dozen good photographs. A dozen is better.

Provide Customer Service. The buyer is likely to need more customer service than in other types of online transactions. Offer it.

Pay Attention to Detail. Vehicle transactions are complex. The buyer will look to you to complete the paperwork and the transaction.

Keep a Cheerful Attitude. No one wants to negotiate with or buy from a sourpuss.

––––––––

This top 8 list will help you focus on what's important for success in selling your vehicle on eBay Motors.

Appendix III Top 9 Tips for Dealers

The top 9 tips for success on eBay for dealers follow below, not necessarily in order of priority:

Read the Top Tips for Sellers. Read the top tips for sellers in another appendix. They are good tips for you too.

Play by the Rules. The eBay rules were set up to make sure that people deal with each other fairly. If you don't play by the eBay rules, you may find eBay Motors to be a hostile marketplace.

Take Advantage of the National Market. eBayMotors provides you with a huge marketplace with which to supplement your local market.

Adjust for Delivery. Adjust your selling price downward for the buyer's cost of taking delivery.

Think of the Buyer. Make it easy for buyers in other cities to buy from you with confidence. About 75 percent of eBay Motors sales take place across state lines.

Create Auction Ads That Sell. When you write your auction ad, give ample and complete information on the vehicle. Post at least a dozen good photographs.

Use Software. Use an auction management service (software delivered via the Web). It makes selling multiple vehicles easier and helps protect your reputation. Specialized eBay Motors auction management services are now available.

Hold a Data Feed Party. This is a euphemism for determining in how many additional online marketplaces you can easily advertise a vehicle to expand your online sales effort.

Tend to Your Reputation (Feedback). For big ticket items, people are less likely to take a chance on sellers with questionable feedback.

———

The top 9 list will help you to develop a healthy selling attitude and start successful sales on eBay Motors.

Appendix IV DMVs

This is a list of the websites of Department of Motor Vehicles (DMV) in each state. Note that they don't all have the name DMV, but go by a variety of names:

General, *http://www.onlinedmv.com/index.html*

Alabama, *http://www.ador.state.al.us/motorvehicle/index.html*

Alaska, *http://www.state.ak.us/local/akpages/ADMIN/ dmv/home.htm*

Arizona, *http://www.dot.state.az.us/MVD/mvd.htm*

Arkansas, *http://www.state.ar.us/dfa/motorvehicle/index.html*

California, *http://www.dmv.ca.gov*

Colorado, *http://www.mv.state.co.us*

Connecticut, *http://www.ct.gov/dmv/site/default.asp*

Delaware, *http://www.delawarepublicsafety.com*

Florida, *http://www.hsmv.state.fl.us*

Georgia, *http://www.dmvs.ga.gov*

Hawaii, *http://www.state.hi.us/dot/highways/index.htm*

Idaho, *http://www2.state.id.us/itd/dmv*

Illinois, *http://www.sos.state.il.us/services/services_motorists.html*

Indiana, *http://www.state.in.us/bmv*

Iowa, *http://www.dot.state.ia.us/mvd/index.htm*

Kansas, *http://www.ksrevenue.org/vehicle.htm*

Kentucky, *http://www.kytc.state.ky.us/mvl*

Louisiana, *http://omv.dps.state.la.us*

Maine, *http://www.state.me.us/sos/bmv*

Maryland, *http://www.mva.state.md.us*

Massachusetts, *http://www.state.ma.us/rmv*

Michigan, *http://www.michigan.gov/sos*

Minnesota, *http://www.dps.state.mn.us/dvs/index.html*

Mississippi, *http://www.mmvc.state.ms.us*

Missouri, *http://www.dor.state.mo.us*

Montana, *http://doj.state.mt.us/department/
motorvehicledivision.asp*

Nebraska, *http://www.dmv.state.ne.us/index.htm*

Nevada, *http://www.dmvnv.com*

New Hampshire, *http://www.nh.gov/safety/dmv*

New Jersey, *http://www.state.nj.us/mvc*

New Mexico, *http://www.state.nm.us/tax/mvd/mvd_home.htm*

New York, *http://www.nydmv.state.ny.us*

North Carolina, *http://www.dmv.dot.state.nc.us*

North Dakota, *http://www.state.nd.us/dot*

Ohio, *http://www.state.oh.us/odps/division/bmv/bmv.html*

Oklahoma, *http://www.oktax.state.ok.us/mvhome.html*

Oregon, *http://www.odot.state.or.us/dmv*

Pennsylvania, *http://www.dot.state.pa.us*

Rhode Island, *http://www.dmv.state.ri.us*

South Carolina, *http://www.scdmvonline.com*

South Dakota, *http://www.state.sd.us/drr2/motorvcl.htm*

Tennessee, *http://www.tennessee.gov/safety/nav2.html*

Texas, *http://www.dot.state.tx.us/txdot.htm*

Utah, *http://dmv.utah.gov*

Vermont, *http://www.aot.state.vt.us/dmv/dmvhp.htm*

Virginia, *http://www.dmv.state.va.us*

Washington, *http://www.dol.wa.gov*

Washington, DC, *http://www.dmv.washingtondc.gov/main.shtm*

West Virginia, *http://www.wvdot.com/6_motorists/dmv/6G_DMV.HTM*

Wisconsin, *http://www.dot.wisconsin.gov/drivers*

Wyoming, *http://wydotweb.state.wy.us*

Index